THE POWER
OF COMPASSION

THE POWER
OF COMPASSION

A Collection of Lectures by
His Holiness the XIV Dalai Lama

Translated by Geshe Thupten Jinpa

Thorsons
An Imprint of HarperCollinsPublishers

Thorsons
An Imprint of HarperCollins*Publishers*
77–85 Fulham Palace Road
Hammersmith, London W6 8JB
1160 Battery Street
San Francisco, California 94111–1213

Published by Thorsons 1995

10 9 8 7 6 5 4 3

© His Holiness the XIV Dalai Lama 1995

His Holiness the XIV Dalai Lama asserts the moral
right to be identified as the author of this work

A catalogue record for this book
is available from the British Library

ISBN 0 7225 3210 5 (Hardback)
ISBN 1 85538 451 5 (Paperback)

Printed in Great Britain by
HarperCollinsManufacturing Glasgow

CONTENTS

PREFACE

His Holiness the Dalai Lama is the head of state and spiritual leader of the Tibetan people. He is also regarded as the world's foremost Buddhist leader and the manifestation of Chenrezig, the Bodhisattva of Compassion.

A scholar and a man of peace, His Holiness the Dalai Lama has travelled the world, not only to raise international awareness of the enormous suffering of the Tibetan people, but also to talk about Buddhism and the power of compassion.

Since 1959 His Holiness has been living in exile in Dharamsala, India, after China's troops crushed a Tibetan National Uprising against Chinese rule in Tibet. China invaded Tibet in 1949/50.

In 1989 His Holiness was awarded the Nobel Peace Prize for his non-violent struggle for the liberation of Tibet. Since coming into exile he has met many of the world's political and spiritual leaders, including President Clinton, Prime Minister John Major, President Vaclav Havel, His Holiness Pope John Paul, the Archbishop of Canterbury and Archbishop Desmond Tutu. He has shared with these leaders his views on human interdependence and his concerns about the arms trade, threats to the environment and intolerance.

His Holiness describes himself as a simple Buddhist monk. In lectures and tours, he disarms audiences with his simplicity, humour and great warmth. Everywhere his message is the same – the importance of love, compassion and forgiveness.

The text for this book is taken from a series of public lectures given by His Holiness the Dalai Lama at Wembley Auditorium in London, England, in May 1993. Although hundreds of people were able to hear these lectures, many people have since asked the Office of Tibet, the official agency of His Holiness the Dalai Lama in London, for transcripts. The Office of Tibet is therefore delighted to be able to offer these words of His Holiness to a world-wide audience.

In the original lectures, His Holiness the Dalai Lama spoke mainly in English, but also to his official translator in Tibetan. The May 1993 visit was sponsored by The Tibet Foundation, London.

The Office of Tibet would like to thank Jane Rasch and Cait Collins for their many hours spent on transcribing the tapes. We would also like to thank His Holiness's translator, Geshe Thupten Jinpa, and Heather Wardle for their work in editing the text into book form.

Kesang Y Takla (Mrs)
Representative of His Holiness the Dalai Lama
London

ONE

CONTENTMENT, JOY AND LIVING WELL

Concerned people have asked me to talk about certain subjects and about the best way to deal with the different situations of life. I will try to explain these things in such a way that ordinary people can see how to utilize their own potential in order to face unpleasant situations, such as death, and also mental frustrations, such as anger and hatred.

I am a Buddhist and my whole way of training is according to the Buddhist teaching or Buddha *Dharma*. Although I speak from my own experience, I feel that no one has the right to impose his or her beliefs on another person. I will not propose to you that my way is best. The decision is up to you. If you find some point which may be suitable for you, then you can carry out experiments for yourself. If you find that it is of no use, then you can discard it.

The basic fact is that all sentient beings, particularly human beings, want happiness and do not want pain and suffering. On those grounds, we have every right to be happy and to use different methods or means to overcome suffering and to achieve happier lives. These methods, however, should not infringe on the rights of others, nor should they create more suffering for others. It is worthwhile to think seriously about the positive and negative consequences of these methods. You should be aware that there are differences between short-term and long-term interests and consequences. If there is a conflict between the short-term interest and the long-term interest, the long-term interest is more important. Buddhists usually say that there is no absolute and that everything is relative. So we must judge according to the circumstances.

Our experiences and feelings are mainly related to our bodies and our minds. We know from our daily experience that mental happiness is beneficial. For instance, though two people may face the same kind of tragedy, one person may face it more easily than the other due to his or her mental attitude.

I believe that the idea that all human problems can be solved by machines or by matter is wrong. Of course, material facilities are extremely useful. At the same time, it is quite natural that all our problems cannot be solved by material facilities alone. In a material society there is just as much mental unrest and frustration, if not more. This shows us that we are human beings after all. We are not the product of machines and our bodies are different from purely mechanical things. Therefore, we must think seriously about our own inner abilities and deeper values.

I believe that if someone really wants a happy life then it is very important to pursue both internal and external means; in other words, material development and mental development. One could also say 'spiritual development', but when I say 'spiritual' I do not necessarily mean any kind of religious faith. When I use the word 'spiritual' I mean basic human good qualities. These are:

human affection, a sense of involvement, honesty, discipline and human intelligence properly guided by good motivation. We have all these things from birth; they do not come to us later in our lives. Religious faith, however, comes later. In this regard, I believe that there are two levels to the various religious teachings. On one level, religious teachings talk about God or the Almighty, or, in Buddhism, about Nirvana and the next life. Yet on a different level, all religious teachings and traditions teach us to be good human beings, to be warm-hearted people. These religious teachings simply strengthen the basic human good qualities which we have from birth.

As humans, we all have the same human potential, unless there is some sort of retarded brain function. The wonderful human brain is the source of our strength and the source of our future, provided we utilize it in the right direction. If we use the brilliant human mind in the wrong way, it is really a disaster. I think human beings are the superior sentient beings on this planet. Humans have the potential not only to create happy lives for themselves, but also to help other beings. We have a natural creative quality and it is very important to realize this.

It is my belief that the human brain and basic human compassion are by nature in some kind of balance. Sometimes, when we grow up, we may neglect human affection and simply concentrate on the human brain, thus losing the balance. It is then that disasters and unwelcome things happen. If we look at different species of mammals, we will see that nature is very important and that it is a forceful factor that creates some sort of balanced way.

With the realization of one's own potential and self-confidence in one's ability, one can build a better world. According to my own experience, self-confidence is very important. That sort of confidence is not a blind one; it is an awareness of one's own potential. On that basis, human beings can transform themselves by increasing the good qualities and reducing the negative qualities. Transformation does not mean 100 per cent change. Without a basis of something to aim for, how do we develop good things? Buddhists call this potential 'Buddha Nature', which is also the fundamental Clear Light nature of the mind.

The fundamental teaching of the Buddha is his teaching on the Four Noble Truths: 1) That there is suffering; 2) that suffering has cause; 3) that there is cessation of suffering; and, finally, that there is a path to such freedom. The underlying principle of this teaching is the universal principle of causality. What becomes important in the understanding of this basic teaching is a genuine awareness of one's own potentials and the need to utilize them to their fullest. Seen in this light, every human action becomes significant.

For example, the smile is a very important feature of the human face. But because of human intelligence, even that good part of human nature can be used in the wrong way, such as sarcastic smiles or diplomatic smiles, which only serve to create suspicion. I feel that a genuine, affectionate smile is very important in our day-to-day lives. How one creates that smile largely depends on one's own attitude. It is illogical to expect smiles from others if one does not smile oneself. Therefore, one can see that many things depend on one's own behaviour.

Now we should talk about our motivation and mental attitude. As I mentioned earlier, the facility which can provide positive things also has the potential for negative things. The important thing is to use human intelligence and judgement, and to be mindful of the benefits for long-term and short-term happiness. Up to a certain point, the body itself is a good indicator. For instance, if some sort of food causes you discomfort one day, then later you will not want to consume that type of food. It seems that at a certain stage the body itself can tell us what is suitable for our well-being and happiness and what is not. For example, on certain days we tend to have a greater wish to eat green salads and certain vegetables, while on other days we may wish to have something else. In a way, these are bodily indications pointing out what is conducive to our constitution and what is not.

While it is very clear, for instance, that when our bodies need more liquid we develop thirst, sometimes our bodies' indications may be confusing. In those instances it is the responsibility of human intelligence to judge what is best. Sometimes your intelligence may oppose your immediate desire because it knows the long-term consequences. Thus, the role of intelligence is to determine the positive and negative potential of an event or factor which could have both positive and negative results. It is the role of intelligence, with the full awareness that is provided by education, to judge and accordingly utilize the potential for one's own benefit or well-being.

If we examine our mental world, we find that there are various mental factors which have both positive and negative aspects. For instance, we can look at two types of mental factors which are quite similar: one is self-confidence and the other is conceit or pride. Both of them are similar in that they are uplifting states of mind which give you a certain degree of confidence and boldness. But conceit and pride tend to lead to more negative consequences, whereas self-confidence tends to lead to more positive consequences. I usually make a distinction between different types of ego. One type of ego is self-cherishing in order to get some benefit for itself, disregarding the rights of others and even taking advantage of others with acts such as killing, stealing and so on. This is the negative ego. Another ego says, 'I must be a good human being. I must serve. I must take full responsibility.' That kind of strong feeling of 'I' or self opposes some of our negative emotions. Unless you have a strong feeling of self-confidence based on a strong self, it is very difficult to do battle with these negative emotions. So there are two types of ego, and wisdom or intelligence makes a distinction. Similarly, we must be able to distinguish between genuine humility and a lack of confidence. One may mistake the two because both of these are sort of slightly humbling mental functions, but one is positive and the other is negative.

Another example of this may be seen if we examine loving kindness and compassion on the one hand, and strong attachment on the other. While both are concerned with an object of endearment, strong attachment tends to lead to negative consequences, whereas love and compassion lead to more positive consequences. Thus two states of mind which show the same basic characteristics can have differing negative and positive results.

Desire is the same. There is both positive and negative desire. I think generally that desire which has proper reasons is positive, whereas desire which has no proper reasons is negative and can lead to problems. Desire is the prime mover in achieving happiness now and for the future. From the Buddhist viewpoint, the attainment of Buddhahood can be achieved only through a certain type of desire. For instance, the Mahayana Buddhist literature mentions two desires or two aspirations. One is the aspiration to be of benefit to all sentient beings and the other is the aspiration to attain fully the Enlightened state for that purpose. Without these two types of aspiration, the attainment of full Enlightenment is not possible. But there are also negative things which result from desire. The antidote to this negative desire is contentment. There are always extremes, but the middle way is the proper way. So if desire pushes you towards the extreme, then your intelligence has the responsibility to check that course and return you to the centre.

The sense of contentment is a key factor for attaining happiness. Bodily health, material wealth and companions and friends are three factors for happiness. Contentment is the key that will determine the outcome of your relations with all three of these factors.

First, with regard to the body, one can see that too much attachment to one's own body sometimes leads to problems. For that reason, Buddhist training looks at the body from a different angle and tries to analyse the nature of the body. To me, thinking along these lines is very useful. I think about the source of my body and the very nature of blood, bones and flesh. The body is not something pure. Even the act of birth is bloody. Also, no matter how beautiful or polished your body appears on the outside, inside there are still a lot of dirty things. With the covering of skin, the human body sometimes looks very beautiful. But if you look more closely, then this body is really quite horrible! Even though we consume good food, with a nice colour, taste and smell, the food is transformed into dirty things. Yet if we try to remove these dirty aspects of the body we cannot survive. And this is the case not only for other people's bodies, but one's own body too. Most importantly, it is because of our bodies that we have illness, old age, pain and death. Yet despite these faults, the body is very precious because of intelligence, which we can use for many great works. Thus, when one's desire or attachment to one's body becomes extreme, it is very effective to meditate on the impure aspects of the body, particularly to reflect on its source, its constitution and its functions, so that one will have a more realistic and moderate outlook on the body.

Similarly, when our attitude towards our material possessions and wealth is not proper, it can lead to an extreme attachment towards such things as our property, houses and belongings. This can lead to an inability to feel contented. If that happens, then one will always remain in a state of dissatisfaction, always wanting more. In a way, one is then really poor, because the suffering of poverty is the suffering of wanting something and feeling the lack of it. So even though one may have a lot of material possessions, if one is mentally poor, then one will always feel lacking and will always want more.

On the other hand, material facilities are quite crucial for society, because when individuals acquire material possessions and develop materially, it contributes in a way to the well-being of the society and the community. For that you need a certain degree of what I would call healthy competition, because without competition perhaps there might not be such good progress and material development. But it is still quite important to be aware of what type of competition we need, which is a sort of friendly competition that would not seek the destruction or the downfall of rivals or other people, but rather would act as a stimulating factor for growth and progress.

Personally, I can see some parallels to the need for competition in material development in spiritual development in Buddhism. In Buddhism, the foundation of the path is taking refuge in the Three Jewels: the Buddha, the *Dharma* and the *sangha* (the spiritual community). The Buddha, being a fully Enlightened being, is very difficult to emulate. You may draw inspiration from the example of the Buddha, but you can't really compete with him, whereas when you take refuge in the *sangha*, the spiritual community, within the community there may be spiritual companions who are at the very beginning of the path to Enlightenment. When you reflect upon the qualities of the *sangha*, then you can get a sense of encouragement – you feel as if you can compete with the others. This is not really a negative competition; it is a healthy competition. Also, you can emulate the example of others ahead of you, with the confidence that you can reach their stage.

Now when we talk about objects of enjoyment or desire and material well-being, Buddhist literature mentions five types of object of desire: form, sound, odours, tastes and tactile sensations. Whether or not these objects of enjoyment give rise to happiness, satisfaction and contentment, or, conversely, give rise to suffering and dissatisfaction depends very much on how you apply your faculty of intelligence.

Similarly, just as in the case of material objects, one's relations to one's friends and companions have different potentials. In some cases, a certain type of interaction with one's friends or companions could lead to additional suffering, frustration and dissatisfaction. A certain type of interaction can also lead to satisfaction, a sense of fulfilment and happiness. Again, the outcome of our interactions depends upon the application of intelligence.

Another important issue is sexual relations. Sexual relations are part of nature and without them there would be no more human beings – that is clear. But to go to the extreme, to a sort of blind love, often creates problems and more misery. I think the main purpose of sexual relations is reproduction, the creation of beautiful new young babies. One must not have just the desire for sexual pleasure, but also a sense of responsibility, a sense of commitment. If we look at other species, I think some are very admirable. For example, certain birds, such as swans, base their relationships solely on a sense of responsibility and they mate for life. This is very beautiful! Some other animals, like dogs, do not have that kind of responsibility and just enjoy the sexual act, leaving the mother with the entire responsibility. This, I think, is awful!

I think as human beings we must follow nature, but the more civilized manner for sexual relations is not to seek just temporary satisfaction. If one does not see the sense of responsibility and marriage, this is short-sighted. Sometimes people ask me about marriage. Of course I have no experience of it, but I am quite sure about one thing: marriage with too much haste is dangerous. First you must have a long period to examine one another and afterwards, when you have genuine confidence that you can live together, then you should marry. That is the proper way.

It seems that many families in these modern times have problems. One reason is that sexual freedom is too extreme. Moreover, part of your modern culture promotes sex and sexual things and I think this is not very healthy. On the other hand, if we compare sex with violence, then I think sex is better! But often because of sex, violence is also created. I think in reality they are very interlinked.

While the most important thing in family life is children, birth control is also extremely important. Of course, from the Buddhist viewpoint, each individual human life is very precious. From that viewpoint, birth control is not good. But at the same time, the world's population is simply getting too great. Perhaps five billion people can be sustained if all the natural resources are utilized properly, and, according to some scientists, another two or three more billion may be acceptable. But I think it is better if we have a smaller number of people; this is more peaceful and more friendly. With this larger interest then, the conclusion is quite clear that we have to use birth control for the benefit of all humanity. Birth control is very necessary.

So, to repeat, our behaviour in our daily lives is the key factor in determining whether all these facilities and relations really produce genuine, long-lasting satisfaction or not. Much depends on our own attitude. And for this mental factor, motivation is the key thing.

In Buddhist literature, human life is seen as a favourable form of existence or rebirth. There are various factors that could complement the favourable existence as a human being, such as having a long life, good health, material possessions and eloquence so that one can relate to others in a more beneficial way. But as I pointed out earlier, whether or not these conditions can lead to a more beneficial existence or to a more harmful one depends very much on how you utilize them and whether or not you apply the faculty of intelligence.

On that point, Buddhist literature mentions the practice of the Six Perfections. For instance, in the case of acquiring material possessions, according to Buddhism, generosity and the act of giving are seen as causes of wealth. But in order to practise generosity and giving successfully, one must first of all have a sound ethical discipline, a certain type of outlook and principles. And that ethical discipline or those principles can come about only if one has the ability to bear hardships and adverse circumstances when confronted with them. For that, you also need a certain degree of exertion or joyful effort. In order to practise the application of joyful effort successfully, one must have the ability to concentrate, to focus on events, actions or goals. That in turn depends on whether or not you have the ability to exercise your power of judgement, to judge between what is desirable and what is undesirable, what is negative and what is positive. So, in a way, all these Six Perfections are related to the acquisition of even one of the conditions, say, material wealth.

How do we go about implementing in our daily lives these principles which are stipulated in the practice of the Six Perfections? Buddhism recommends living one's life within the ethical discipline of observance of what are known as the Ten Precepts, or Avoidance of the Ten Negative Actions. Out of these Ten Negative Actions, one, known as 'wrong views' or 'perverted views', might make more sense within the context of a religious belief. Other than that, all the other

FACING DEATH AND DYING WELL

The issue of facing death in a peaceful manner is a very difficult one. According to common sense, there seems to be two ways of dealing with the problem and the suffering. The first is simply to try to avoid the problem, to put it out of your mind, even though the reality of that problem is still there and it is not minimized. Another way of dealing with this issue is to look directly at the problem and analyse it, make it familiar to you and make it clear that it is a part of all our lives.

I have already touched on the topic of the body and illness. Illness happens. It is not something exceptional; it is part of nature and a fact of life. It happens because the body is there. Of course we have every right to avoid illness and pain, but in spite of that effort, when illness happens it is better to accept it. While you should make every effort to cure it as soon as possible, you should have no extra mental burden. As the great Indian scholar Shantideva has said: 'If there is a way to overcome the suffering, then there is no need to worry; if there is no way to overcome the suffering, then there is no use in worrying.' That kind of rational attitude is quite useful.

Now I want to speak about death. Death is a part of all our lives. Whether we like it or not, it is bound to happen. Instead of avoiding thinking about it, it is better to understand its meaning. On the news we often see murders and death, but some people seem to think that death happens only to others, not to themselves. That kind of attitude is wrong. We all have the same body, the same human flesh, and therefore we will all die. There is a big difference, of course, between natural death and accidental death, but basically death will come sooner or later. If from the beginning your attitude is, 'Yes, death is part of our lives', then it may be easier to face.

So there are two distinct approaches to

dealing with a problem. One is to simply avoid it by not thinking about it. The other, which is much more effective, is to face it directly so that you are already conscious of it. Generally, there are two types of problem or suffering: with one type, it is possible that, by adopting a certain attitude, one will be able to actually reduce the force and level of suffering and anxiety. However, there could be other types of problem and suffering for which adopting a certain type of attitude and way of thinking may not necessarily reduce the level of suffering, but which would still prepare you to face it.

When unfortunate things happen in our lives there are two possible results. One possibility is mental unrest, anxiety, fear, doubt, frustration and eventually depression, and, in the worst case, even suicide. That's one way. The other possibility is that because of that tragic experience you become more realistic, you become closer to reality. With the power of investigation, the tragic experience may make you stronger and increase your self-confidence and self-reliance. The unfortunate event can be a source of inner strength.

The success of our lives and our futures, as I have said, depends on our individual motivation and determination or self-confidence. Through difficult experiences, life sometimes becomes more meaningful. If you look at people who, from the beginning of their lives, have had everything, you may see that when small things happen they soon lose hope or grow irritated. Others, like the generation of people in England who experienced World War II, have developed stronger mental attitudes as a result of their hardships. I think the person who has had more experience of hardships can stand more firmly in the face of problems than the person who has never experienced suffering. From this angle then, some suffering can be a good lesson for life.

Now is this attitude just a way of deceiving oneself? Personally, I have lost my country and, worse still, in my country there has been a lot of destruction, suffering and unhappiness. I have spent not only the majority of my life but also the best part of my life outside Tibet. If you think of this from that angle alone, there is hardly anything that is positive. But from another angle, you can see that because of these unfortunate things I have had another type of freedom, such as the opportunity of meeting different people from different traditions and also of meeting scientists from different fields. From those experiences my life has been enriched and I have learned many valuable things. So my tragic experiences have also had some valuable aspects.

Looking at problems from these different angles actually lessens the mental burden or mental frustration. From the Buddhist viewpoint, every event has many aspects and naturally one event can be viewed from many, many different angles. It is very rare or almost impossible that an event can be negative from all points of view. Therefore, it is useful when something happens to try to look at it from different angles and then you can see the positive or beneficial aspects. Moreover, if something happens, it is very useful immediately to make a comparison with some other event or with the events of other people or other nations. This is also very helpful in sustaining your peace of mind.

I will now explain, as a Buddhist monk, how to deal with death. Buddha taught the principles of the Four Noble Truths, the first of which is the Truth of Suffering. The Truth of Suffering is taught within the context of three characteristics of existence, the first being impermanence. When talking about the nature of impermanence we must bear in mind that there are two levels. One is the coarse level, which is quite obvious and is the cessation of the continuation of a life or an event. But the impermanent nature which is being taught in relation to the Four Noble Truths refers to the more subtle aspect of impermanence, which is the transitory nature of existence.

Buddha's teaching of the more subtle aspects of the impermanent nature of existence aims at establishing an appreciation of the basic unsatisfactory nature of our existence. If you understand the nature of impermanence correctly, you will understand that it reveals that any existents which are causally produced, that is, which come about as a result of causes and conditions, entirely depend on causes and conditions for their existence.

26

Not only that, but the very causes and conditions which have produced them also bring about the disintegration and cessation of those very entities. So, within the seed of the cause of events is the seed for their cessation and disintegration. When this is related to the understanding of the impermanent nature of our own aggregates, the body and mind, then here the cause refers to our own ignorant state of mind, which is the root of our existence, and this reveals that our very physical existence, our bodily existence, is very much governed by the force of an ignorant state of mind.

But it is by first reflecting upon the coarser levels of impermanence that one is eventually led to an appreciation of the subtle levels of impermanence. And by this, one will be able to confront and counteract grasping at permanence or eternal existence of one's own identity or self, because it is this grasping at permanence that forces us to cling onto this very 'now-ness' or matters of one's lifetime alone. By releasing the grip of this grasping and enduring within us, we will be in a better position to appreciate the value of working for our future lifetimes.

One of the reasons why awareness of death and impermanence is so crucial in the Buddhist religious practice is that it is considered that your state of mind at the time of death has a very great effect on determining what form of rebirth you might take. Whether it is a positive state of mind or a negative one will have a great effect. Therefore, Buddhist religious practice greatly emphasizes the importance of the awareness of death and impermanence.

Although the main purpose of a high degree of awareness of impermanence is to train oneself so that at the time of death one will be in a virtuous and positive state of mind and will be assured of a positive rebirth, there are other benefits. One of the positive side-effects of maintaining a very high degree of awareness of death is that it will prepare the individual to such an extent that, when the individual actually faces death, he or she will be in a better position to maintain his or her presence of mind. Especially in Tantric Buddhism, it is considered that the state of mind which one experiences at the point of death is extremely subtle and, because of the subtlety of the level of that consciousness, it also has a great power and impact upon one's mental continuum. So in Tantric practices we find a lot of emphasis placed on death-related meditations and also reflections upon the process of death, so that the individual at the time of death not only retains his or her presence of mind, but also is in a position to utilize that subtle state of consciousness effectively towards the realization of the path.

It is because of this that we find many Tantric meditations, technically known as the 'deity yoga meditations' because they are meditations on deities, involve the dissolution process, reflecting upon the dissolution of elements which the individual experiences at the point of death. In fact, from the Tantric perspective, the entire process of existence is explained in terms of the three stages known as 'death', 'the intermediate state' and 'rebirth'. All of these three stages of existence are seen as states or manifestations of the consciousness and the energies that accompany or propel the consciousness, so that the intermediate state and rebirth are nothing other than various levels of the subtle consciousness and energy. An example of such fluctuating states can be found in our daily existence, when during the 24-hour day we go through a cycle of deep sleep, the waking period and the dream state. Our daily existence is in fact characterized by these three stages.

When talking about the distinctions that are made in the Tantric literature between the subtle and gross levels of consciousness and mind, I think it is important to bear in mind what exactly we mean by 'mental consciousness'. Often people get the impression that when we talk about the sixth mental consciousness there is some kind of autonomous type of consciousness which is totally independent from the bodily states and which is, in a way, the equivalent of the soul. But this is a misunderstanding. I personally think that if we were to examine our mental world we would find that most of our mental states and mental functions have direct physical correlates. Not only the sensory consciousness, but also much of what we would call mental consciousness has physiological bases and is intimately linked with the bodily states, just as scientists would say that the brain and nervous system are the primary physiological bases of much of our conscious experience. Therefore, when the bodily states cease, these mental functions also cease.

But the question really is: what makes it possible for certain physical substances or physiological states to give rise to a mental event or a state of awareness? The Buddhist, particularly the Tantric, explanation points towards what is known as the subtle Clear Light state, which can be seen as independent from a physiological base. And it is this Clear Light state of mind which is the most subtle level of consciousness and which, when it interacts with the physiological base, gives rise to all our conscious and cognitive events.

There are certain indications of the existence of what we call the Clear Light state of mind. There are incidents which generally tend to be more possible for religious practitioners. For instance, among the Tibetan community in exile there have been cases where people have been pronounced clinically dead, that is, their brain function has ceased and the brain is dead but the decomposition of the body has not begun, and they remain in that state for days on end. For instance, my own late tutor, Kyabje Ling Rinpoche, remained in that state for 13 days. He was pronounced clinically dead and he had already experienced the death of the brain, but his body remained fresh and did not decompose for 13 days.

Now there must be some explanation for this. The Buddhist explanation is that, during that state, the individual is not actually dead but rather in the process of dying. Buddhists would explain that although the mind–body relationship may have ceased at the grosser, coarse level, it has not ceased at the subtle level. According to particular Tantric literature known as the *Guhyasamaja Tantra*, when an individual goes through the process of death, there is a certain process of dissolution. From that dissolution into the Clear Light state there is a reversal cycle and when that cycle reaches a certain stage, a new life begins that is called the rebirth. Then that rebirth remains and the individual again goes through a process of dissolution. In a way, death is at the intervening stage when the elements dissolve into the Clear Light and from there re-arise in another form. So death is nothing other than these intervening points when the individual's various physiological elements dissolve into the Clear Light point.

As regards the actual dissolution process of the various elements, the literature mentions different stages of dissolution and their accompanying signs. For instance, in the case of the dissolution of the coarser levels of elements, there are both internal and external signs and indications that mark the dissolution. When it comes to the subtle elements, there are only internal signs such as visions and so forth. There has been a growing interest among scientists who are doing research on death in these descriptions of the dissolution processes, particularly the internal and external signs. As a Buddhist, I think it is very important for us to be aware of the scientific investigations that are being undertaken. However, we must be able to distinguish between phenomena which still remain beyond the verification of existing scientific methodology and phenomena which can be seen as being disproved by existing scientific methods and investigation. I would say that if certain phenomena can be seen as being disproved by science, through scientific investigation and scientific methods, I think as Buddhists we will have to respect those conclusions.

As death becomes something familiar to you, as you have some knowledge of its processes and can recognize its external and internal indications, you are prepared for it. According to my own experience, I still have no confidence that at the moment of death I will really implement all these practices for which I have prepared. I have no guarantee! However, sometimes when I think about death I get some kind of excitement. Instead of fear, I have a feeling of curiosity and this makes it much easier for me to accept death. I wonder to what extent I can implement these practices. Of course, my only burden if I die today is, 'Oh, what will happen to Tibet? What about Tibetan culture? What about the six million Tibetan people's rights?' This is my main concern. Otherwise, I feel almost no fear of death. Perhaps I have some kind of blind confidence! So it is good to reduce the fear of death. In my daily practice of prayer I visualize eight different deity yogas and eight different deaths. Perhaps when death comes all my preparation may fail. I hope not!

Anyway, I think that way is mentally very helpful in dealing with death. Even if there is no next life, there is some benefit if it relieves fear. And because there is less fear, one can be more fully prepared. Just as for battle, without preparation there is a good chance you will lose, but if you are fully prepared, there is more chance of defence. If you are fully prepared then, at the moment of death, you can retain your peace of mind. It is peace of mind at the time of death which is the foundation for cultivating the proper motivation and that is the immediate guarantee of a good rebirth, of a better life to come. Particularly for the practitioner of the Maha-anuttarayoga Tantrayana, death is one of the rare opportunities to transform the subtle mind into wisdom.

As to what is in store for us after death, Buddhists talk about three realms of existence, technically known as 'the form realm', 'the formless realm' and 'the desire realm'. Both the form realm and the desire realm have an intervening stage before you take rebirth, known as 'the intermediate state'. What all of this points towards is that although the occasion of death provides us with the best opportunity to utilize our most subtle level of consciousness, transforming it into a path of wisdom, even if we are not able to seize that opportunity effectively, there is an intermediate state which, though grosser than at the time of death, is a lot more subtle than the consciousness at the time of rebirth. So there is another opportunity. And even if we are unable to seize this opportunity, there is rebirth and a continuing cycle.

So in order to seize the wonderful opportunity accorded at the time of death and, after that, during the intermediate state, we need first to train ourselves to be able to utilize those moments. For that, Buddhism teaches various techniques to enable the individual to apply certain meditative techniques during each of the dream, deep sleep and waking states.

In conclusion, I think at the time of death a peaceful mind is essential no matter what you believe in, whether it is Buddhism or some other religion. At the moment of death, the individual should not seek to develop anger, hatred and so on. That is very important at the conventional level. I think even non-believers see that it is better to pass away in a peaceful manner. It is much happier. Also, for those who believe in heaven or some other concept, it is also best to pass away peacefully with the thought of one's own God or belief in higher forces. For Buddhists and also other ancient Indian traditions which accept the rebirth or karma theory, naturally at the time of death a virtuous state of mind is beneficial.

THREE

DEALING WITH ANGER AND EMOTION

Anger and hatred are two of our closest friends. When I was young I had quite a close relationship with anger. Then eventually I found a lot of disagreement with anger. By using common sense, with the help of compassion and wisdom, I now have a more powerful argument with which to defeat anger.

According to my experience, it is clear that if each individual makes an effort then he or she can change. Of course, change is not immediate and it takes a lot of time. In order to change and deal with emotions it is crucial to analyse which thoughts are useful, constructive and of benefit to us. I mean mainly those thoughts which make us calmer, more relaxed and which give us peace of mind, versus those thoughts which create uneasiness, fear and frustration. This analysis is

similar to one which we might use for external things, such as plants. Some plants,
flowers and fruit are good for us, so we use
them and grow them. Those plants which are
poisonous or harmful to us, we learn to recognize and even sometimes to destroy.

There is a similarity with the inner world.
It is too simplistic to speak about the 'body'
and the 'mind'. Within the body there are billions of different particles. Similarly, there
are many different thoughts and a variety of
states of mind. It is wise to take a close look
into the world of your mind and to make the
distinction between beneficial and harmful
states of mind. Once you can recognize the
value of good states of mind, you can increase
or foster them.

Buddha taught the principles of the Four
Noble Truths and these form the foundation
of the Buddha *Dharma*. The Third Noble
Truth is cessation. According to Nagarjuna,
in this context cessation means the state of
mind or mental quality which, through practice and effort, ceases all the negative emotions. Nagarjuna defines true cessation as a
state in which the individual has reached a

perfected state of mind which is free from the effects of various afflictive and negative emotions and thoughts. Such a state of true cessation is, according to Buddhism, a genuine *Dharma* and therefore is the refuge that all practising Buddhists seek. Buddha becomes an object of refuge, worthy of respect, because Buddha has realized that state. Therefore one's reverence to the Buddha, and the reason one seeks refuge in the Buddha, is not because Buddha was from the beginning a special person, but because Buddha realized the state of true cessation. Similarly, the spiritual community, or *sangha*, is taken as an object of refuge because the members of the spiritual community are individuals who are either already on, or are embarking on, the path leading to that state of cessation.

We find that the true state of cessation can be understood only in terms of a state of mind which is free from, or which has been purified of, negative emotions and thoughts due to the application of antidotes and counter-forces. True cessation is a state of mind and the factors that lead to this are also functions of the mind. Also, the basis on which the purification takes place is the mental continuum. Therefore, an understanding of the nature of the mind is crucial for Buddhist practice. By saying this, I do not mean that everything which exists is simply a reflection or projection of the mind and that apart from the mind nothing exists. But because of the importance of understanding the nature of mind in Buddhist practice, people often describe Buddhism as 'a science of the mind'.

Generally speaking, in Buddhist literature, a negative emotion or thought is defined as 'a state which causes disturbance within one's mind'. These afflictive emotions and thoughts are factors that create unhappiness and turmoil within us. Emotion in general is not necessarily something negative. At a scientific conference which I attended along with many psychologists and neuro-scientists, it was concluded that even Buddhas have emotion, according to the definition of emotion found in various scientific disciplines. So *karuna* (infinite compassion or kindness) can be described as a kind of emotion.

Naturally, emotions can be positive and

negative. However, when talking about anger, etc., we are dealing with negative emotions. Negative emotions are those which immediately create some kind of unhappiness or uneasiness and which, in the long run, create certain actions. Those actions ultimately lead to harm to others and this brings pain or suffering to oneself. This is what we mean by negative emotions.

One negative emotion is anger. Perhaps there are two types of anger. One type of anger could be transformed into a positive emotion. For example, if one has a sincere compassionate motivation and concern for someone and that person does not heed one's warning about his or her actions, then there is no other alternative except the use of some kind of force to stop that person's misdeeds. In Tantrayana practice there are meditative techniques which enable the transformation of the energy of anger. This is the reason behind the wrathful deities. On the basis of compassionate motivation, anger may in some cases be useful because it gives us extra energy and enables us to act swiftly.

However, anger usually leads to hatred and

hatred is always negative. Hatred harbours ill will. I usually analyse anger on two levels: on the basic human level and on the Buddhist level. From the human level, without any reference to a religious tradition or ideology, we can look at the sources of our happiness: good health, material facilities and good companions. Now from the stand-point of health, negative emotions such as hatred are very bad. Since people generally try to take care of their health, one technique people can use is their mental attitude. Your mental state should always remain calm. Even if some anxiety occurs, as it is bound to in life, you should always be calm. Like a wave, which rises from the water and dissolves back into the water, these disturbances are very short, so they should not affect your basic mental attitude. Though you cannot eliminate all negative emotions, if your basic mental attitude is healthy and calm, it will not be much affected. If you remain calm your blood pressure and so on remains more normal and as a result your health will improve. While I cannot say scientifically why this is so, I believe that my own physical condition is improving as I get older. I have had the same medicine, the same doctor, the same food, so it must be due to my mental state. Some people say to me, 'You must have some kind of special Tibetan medicine.' But I don't!

As I mentioned earlier, when I was young I was quite short-tempered. I would sometimes excuse this by saying that it was because my father was short-tempered, as if it was something genetic. But as time passes, I think that now I have almost no hatred towards anybody, including towards those Chinese who are creating misery and suffering for Tibetans. Even towards them, I really do not feel any kind of hatred.

Some of my close friends have high blood pressure, yet they never come near to having crises in their health and they never feel tired. Over the years I have met some very good practitioners. Meanwhile, there are other friends who have great material comfort yet, when we start to talk, after the initial few nice words, they begin to complain and grieve. In spite of their material prosperity, these people do not have calm or peaceful minds. As a result, they are always worrying about their digestion, their sleep, everything! Therefore it is clear that mental calmness is a very important factor for good health. If you want good health, don't ask a doctor, look within yourself. Try to utilize some of your potential. This even costs less!

The second source of happiness is material facilities. Sometimes when I wake up in the early morning, if my mood is not very good, then when I look at my watch I feel uncomfortable because of my mood. Then on other days, due perhaps to the previous day's experience, when I wake up my mood is pleasant and peaceful. At that time, when I look at my watch I see it as extraordinarily beautiful. Yet it is the same watch, isn't it? The difference comes from my mental attitude. Whether our use of our material facilities provides genuine satisfaction or not depends on our mental attitude.

It is bad for our material facilities if our mind is dominated by anger. To speak again from my own experience, when I was young I sometimes repaired watches. I tried and failed many times. Sometimes I would lose my patience and hit the watch! During those moments, my anger altered my whole attitude and afterwards I felt very sorry for my actions. If my goal was to repair the watch, then why did I hit it on the table? Again you can see how one's mental attitude is crucial in order to utilize material facilities for one's genuine satisfaction or benefit.

The third source of happiness is our companions. It is obvious that when you are mentally calm you are honest and open-minded. I will give you an example. Perhaps 14 or 15 years ago, there was an Englishman named Phillips, who had a close relationship with the Chinese government, including with Chou En Lai and other leaders. He had known them for many years and he was close friends with the Chinese. One time, in 1977 or 1978, Phillips came to Dharamsala to see me. He brought some films with him and he told me about all the good aspects of China. At the beginning of our meeting there was a big disagreement between us, for we held completely different opinions. In his view, the presence of the Chinese in Tibet was something good. In my opinion, and according to many reports, the situation was not good. As usual, I had no particular negative feeling towards him. I just felt that he held these views due to ignorance. With openness, I continued our conversation. I argued that those Tibetans who had joined the Chinese Communist Party as early as 1930 and who had participated in the Sino–Japanese War and had welcomed the Chinese invasion and enthusiastically collaborated with the Chinese Communists did so because they believed that it was a golden opportunity to develop Tibet, from the viewpoint of Marxist ideology. These people had collaborated with the Chinese out of genuine hope. Then around 1956 or 1957 most of them were dismissed from the various Chinese offices, some were imprisoned and others disappeared. Thus I explained that we are not anti-Chinese or anti-Communist. In fact, I sometimes think of myself as a half-Marxist, half-Buddhist. I explained all these different things to him with sincere motivation and openness and after some time his attitude completely changed. This instance gives me some confirmation that even if there is a big difference of opinion, you can communicate on a human level. You can put aside these different opinions and communicate as human beings. I think that is one way to create positive feelings in other people's minds.

Also, I am quite sure that if this Fourteenth Dalai Lama smiled less, perhaps I would have fewer friends in various places. My attitude towards other people is to always look at them from the human level. On that level, whether president, queen or beggar, there is no difference, provided that there is genuine human feeling with a genuine human smile of affection.

I think that there is more value in genuine human feeling than in status and so on. I am just a simple human being. Through my experience and mental discipline, a certain new attitude has developed. This is nothing special. You, who I think have had a better education and more experience than myself, have more potential to change within yourself. I come from a small village with no modern education and no deep awareness of the world. Also, from the age of 15 or 16 I had an unthinkable sort of burden. Therefore each of you should feel that you have great potential and that, with self-confidence and a little more effort, change really is possible if you want it. If you feel that your present way of life is unpleasant or has some difficulties, then don't look at these negative things. See the positive side, the potential, and make an effort. I think that there is already at that point some kind of partial guarantee of success. If we utilize all our positive human energy or human qualities we can overcome these human problems.

So, as far as our contact with fellow human beings is concerned, our mental attitude is very crucial. Even for a non-believer, just a simple honest human being, the ultimate source of happiness is in our mental attitude. Even if you have good health, material facilities used in the proper way and good relations with other human beings, the main cause of a happy life is within. If you have more money you sometimes have more worries and you still feel hungry for more. Ultimately you become a slave of money. While money is very useful and necessary, it is not the ultimate source of happiness. Similarly, education, if not well balanced, can sometimes create more trouble, more anxiety, more greed, more desire and more ambition – in short, more mental suffering. Friends, too, are sometimes very troublesome.

Now you can see how to minimize anger and hatred. First, it is extremely important to realize the negativeness of these emotions in general, particularly hatred. I consider hatred to be the ultimate enemy. By 'enemy' I mean the person or factor which directly or indirectly destroys our interest. Our interest is that which ultimately creates happiness.

We can also speak of the external enemy. For example, in my own case, our Chinese brothers and sisters are destroying Tibetan rights and, in that way, more suffering and anxiety develops. But no matter how forceful this is, it cannot destroy the supreme source of my happiness, which is my calmness of mind. This is something an external enemy cannot destroy. Our country can be invaded, our possessions can be destroyed, our friends can be killed, but these are secondary for our mental happiness. The ultimate source of my mental happiness is my peace of mind. Nothing can destroy this except my own anger.

Moreover, you can escape or hide from an external enemy and sometimes you can even cheat the enemy. For example, if there is someone who disturbs my peace of mind, I can escape by locking my door and sitting quietly alone. But I cannot do that with anger! Wherever I go, it is always there. Even though I have locked my room, the anger is still inside. Unless you adopt a certain method, there is no possibility of escape. Therefore, hatred or anger – and here I mean negative anger – is ultimately the real destroyer of my peace of mind and is therefore my true enemy.

Some people believe that to suppress emotion is not good, that it is much better to let it out. I think there are differences between various negative emotions. For example, with frustration, there is a certain frustration which develops as a result of past events. Sometimes if you hide these negative events, such as sexual abuse, then consciously or unconsciously this creates problems. Therefore, in this case it is much better to express the frustration and let it out. However, according to our experience with anger, if you do not make an attempt to reduce it, it will remain with you and even increase. Then even with small incidents you will immediately get angry. Once you try to control or discipline your anger, then eventually even big events will not cause anger. Through training and discipline you can change.

When anger comes there is one important technique to help you keep your peace of mind. You should not become dissatisfied or frustrated, because this is the cause of anger and hatred. There is a natural connection between cause and effect. Once certain causes and conditions are fully met, it is extremely difficult to prevent that causal process from coming to fruition. It is crucial to examine the situation so that at a very early stage one is able to put a stop to the causal process. Then it does not continue to an advanced stage. In the Buddhist text *Guide to the Bodhisattva Way of Life*, the great scholar Shantideva mentions that it is very important to ensure that a person does not get into a situation which leads to dissatisfaction, because dissatisfaction is the seed of anger. This means that one must adopt a certain outlook towards one's material possessions, towards one's companions and friends, and towards various situations.

Our feelings of dissatisfaction, unhappiness, loss of hope and so forth are in fact related to all phenomena. If we do not adopt the right outlook, it is possible that anything and everything could cause us frustration. For some people even the name of the Buddha could conceivably cause anger and frustration, although it may not be the case when someone has a direct personal encounter with a Buddha. Therefore, all phenomena have the potential to create frustration and dissatisfaction in us. Yet phenomena are part of reality and we are subject to the laws of existence. So this leaves us only one option: to change our own attitude. By bringing about a change in our outlook towards things and events, all phenomena can become friends or sources of happiness, instead of becoming enemies or sources of frustration.

A particular case is that of an enemy. Of course, in one way, having an enemy is very bad. It disturbs our mental peace and destroys some of our good things. But if we look at it from another angle, only an enemy gives us the opportunity to practise patience. No one else provides us with the opportunity for tolerance. For example, as a Buddhist, I think Buddha completely failed to provide us with the opportunity to practise tolerance and patience. Some members of the *sangha* may provide us with this, but otherwise it is quite rare. Since we do not know the majority of the five billion human beings on this earth, therefore the majority of people do not give us an opportunity to show tolerance or patience either. Only those people whom we know and who create problems for us really provide us with a good opportunity to practise tolerance and patience.

Seen from this angle, the enemy is the greatest teacher for our practice. Shantideva argues very brilliantly that enemies, or the perpetrators of harm upon us, are in fact objects worthy of respect and are worthy of being regarded as our precious teachers. One might object that our enemies cannot be considered worthy of our respect because they have no intention of helping us; the fact that they are helpful and beneficial to us is merely a coincidence. Shantideva says that if this is the case then why should we, as practising Buddhists, regard the state of cessation as an object worthy of refuge when cessation is a mere state of mind and on its part has no intention of helping us. One may then say that although this is true, at least with cessation there is no intention of harming us, whereas enemies, contrary to having the intention of helping us, in fact intend to harm us. Therefore an enemy is not an object worthy of respect. Shantideva says that it is this very intention of harming us which makes the enemy very special. If the enemy had no intention of harming us, then we would not classify that person as an enemy, therefore our attitude would be completely different. It is his or her very intention of harming us which makes that person an enemy and because of that the enemy provides us with an opportunity to practise tolerance and patience. Therefore an enemy is indeed a precious teacher. By thinking along these lines you can eventually reduce the negative mental emotions, particularly hatred.

Sometimes people feel that anger is useful because it brings extra energy and boldness. When we encounter difficulties, we may see anger as a protector. But though anger brings us more energy, that energy is essentially a blind one. There is no guarantee that that anger and energy will not become destructive to our own interests. Therefore hatred and anger are not at all useful.

Another question is that if you always remain humble then others may take advantage of you and how should you react? It is quite simple: you should act with wisdom or common sense, without anger and hatred. If the situation is such that you need some sort of action on your part, you can, without anger, take a counter-measure. In fact, such actions which follow true wisdom rather than anger are in reality more effective. A counter-measure taken in the midst of anger may often go wrong. In a very competitive society, it is sometimes necessary to take a counter-measure. We can again examine the Tibetan situation. As I mentioned earlier, we are following a genuinely non-violent and compassionate way, but this does not mean that we should just bow down to the aggressors' action and give in. Without anger and without hatred, we can manage more effectively.

There is another type of practice of tolerance which involves consciously taking on the sufferings of others. I am thinking of situations in which, by engaging in certain activities, we are aware of the hardships, difficulties and problems that are involved in the short term, but are convinced that such actions will have a very beneficial long-term effect. Because of our attitude and our commitment and wish to bring about that long-term benefit, we sometimes consciously and deliberately take upon ourselves the hardships and problems that are involved in the short term.

One of the effective means by which one can overcome the forces of negative emotions like anger and hatred is by cultivating their counter-forces, such as the positive qualities of mind like love and compassion.

FOUR

GIVING AND RECEIVING:

*A Practical Way of Directing Love
and Compassion*

Compassion is the most wonderful and precious thing. When we talk about compassion, it is encouraging to note that basic human nature is, I believe, compassionate and gentle. Sometimes I argue with friends who believe that human nature is more negative and aggressive. I argue that if you study the structure of the human body you will see that it is akin to those species of mammals whose way of life is more gentle or peaceful. Sometimes I half joke that our hands are arranged in such a manner that they are good for hugging, rather than hitting. If our hands were mainly meant for hitting, then these beautiful fingers would not be necessary. For example, if the fingers remain extended, boxers cannot hit forcefully, so they have to make fists. So I think that means that our basic physical structure creates a compassionate or gentle kind of nature.

If we look at relationships, marriage and conception are very important. As I said earlier, marriage should not be based on blind love or an extreme sort of mad love; it should be based on a knowledge of one another and an understanding that you are suitable to live together. Marriage is not for temporary satisfaction, but for some kind of sense of responsibility. That is the genuine love which is the basis of marriage.

The proper conception of a child takes place in that kind of moral or mental attitude. While the child is in the mother's womb, the mother's calmness of mind has a very positive effect on the unborn child, according to some scientists. If the mother's mental state is negative, for instance if she is frustrated or angry, then it is very harmful to the healthy development of the unborn child. One scientist has told me that the first few weeks after birth is the most important period, for during that time the child's brain is enlarging. During that period, the mother's touch or that of someone who is acting like a mother is crucial. This shows that even though the child may not realize who is who, it somehow physically needs someone else's affection. Without that, it is very damaging for the healthy development of the brain.

After birth, the first act by the mother is to give the child nourishing milk. If the mother lacks affection or kind feelings for the child, then the milk will not flow. If the mother feeds her baby with gentle feelings towards the child, in spite of her own illness or pain, as a result the milk flows freely. This kind of attitude is like a precious jewel. Moreover, from the other side, if the child lacks some kind of close feeling towards the mother, it may not suckle. This shows how wonderful the act of affection from both sides is. That is the beginning of our lives.

Similarly with education, it is my experience that those lessons which we learn from teachers who are not just good, but who also show affection for the student, go deep into our minds. Lessons from other sorts of teachers may not. Although you may be compelled to study and may fear the teacher, the lessons may not sink in. Much depends on the affection from the teacher.

Likewise, when we go to a hospital, irrespective of the doctor's quality, if the doctor shows genuine feeling and deep concern for us, and if he or she smiles, then we feel OK. But if the doctor shows little human affection, then even though he or she may be a very great expert, we may feel unsure and nervous. This is human nature.

Lastly, we can reflect on our lives. When we are young and again when we are old, we depend heavily on the affection of others. Between these stages we usually feel that we can do everything without help from others and that other people's affection is simply not important. But at this stage I think it is very important to keep deep human affection. When people in a big town or city feel lonely, this does not mean that they lack human companions, but rather that they lack human affection. As a result of this, their mental health eventually becomes very poor. On the other hand, those people who grow up in an atmosphere of human affection have a much more positive and gentle development of their bodies, their minds and their behaviour.

Children who have grown up lacking that atmosphere usually have more negative attitudes. This very clearly shows the basic human nature. Also, as I have mentioned, the human body appreciates peace of mind. Things that are disturbing to us have a very bad effect upon our health. This shows that the whole structure of our health is such that it is suited to an atmosphere of human affection. Therefore, our potential for compassion is there. The only issue is whether or not we realize this and utilize it.

The basic aim of my explanation is to show that by nature we are compassionate, that compassion is something very necessary and something which we can develop. It is important to know the exact meaning of compassion. Different philosophies and traditions have different interpretations of the meaning of love and compassion. Some of my Christian friends believe that love cannot develop without God's grace; in other words, to develop love and compassion you need faith. The Buddhist interpretation is that genuine compassion is based on a clear acceptance or recognition that others, like oneself, want happiness and have the right to overcome suffering. On that basis one develops some kind of concern about the welfare of others, irrespective of one's attitude to oneself. That is compassion.

Your love and compassion towards your friends is in many cases actually attachment. This feeling is not based on the realization that all beings have an equal right to be happy and to overcome suffering. Instead, it is based on the idea that something is 'mine', 'my friend' or something good for 'me'. That is attachment. Thus, when that person's attitude towards you changes, your feeling of closeness immediately disappears. With the other way, you develop some kind of concern irrespective of the other person's attitude to you, simply because that person is a fellow human being and has every right to overcome suffering. Whether that person remains neutral to you or even becomes your enemy, your concern should remain because of his or her right. That is the main difference. Genuine compassion is much healthier; it is unbiased and it is based on reason. By contrast, attachment is narrow-minded and biased.

Actually, genuine compassion and attachment are contradictory. According to Buddhist practice, to develop genuine compassion you must first practise the meditation of equalization and equanimity, detaching oneself from those people who are very close to you. Then, you must remove negative feelings towards your enemies. All sentient beings should be looked on as equal. On that basis, you can gradually develop genuine compassion for all of them. It must be said that genuine compassion is not like pity or a feeling that others are somehow lower than yourself. Rather, with genuine compassion you view others as more important than yourself.

As I pointed out earlier, in order to generate genuine compassion, first of all one must go through the training of equanimity. This becomes very important because without a sense of equanimity towards all, one's feelings towards others will be biased. So now I will give you a brief example of a Buddhist meditative training on developing equanimity. You should think about, first, a small group of people whom you know, such as your friends and relatives, towards whom you have attachment. Second, you should think about some people to whom you feel totally indifferent. And third, think about some people whom you dislike. Once you have imagined these different people, you should try to let your mind go into its natural state and see how it would normally respond to an encounter with these people. You will notice that your natural reaction would be that of attachment towards your friends, that of dislike towards the people whom you consider enemies and that of total indifference towards those whom you consider neutral. Then you should try to question yourself. You should compare the effects of the two opposing attitudes you have towards your friends and your enemies, and see why you should have such fluctuating states of mind towards these two different groups of people. You should see what effects such reactions have on your mind and try to see the futility of relating to them in such an extreme manner. I have already discussed the pros and cons of harbouring hatred and generating anger towards enemies, and I have also spoken a little about the defects of being extremely attached towards friends and so on. You should reflect upon this and then try to minimize your strong emotions towards these two opposing groups of people. Then, most importantly, you should reflect on the fundamental equality between yourself and all other sentient beings. Just as you have the instinctive natural desire to be happy and overcome suffering, so do all sentient beings; just as you have the right to fulfil this innate aspiration, so do all sentient beings. So on what exact grounds do you discriminate?

If we look at humanity as a whole, we are social animals. Moreover, the structures of the modern economy, education and so on, illustrate that the world has become a smaller place and that we heavily depend on one another. Under such circumstances, I think the only option is to live and work together harmoniously and keep in our minds the interest of the whole of humanity. That is the only outlook and way we must adopt for our survival.

By nature, especially as a human being, my interests are not independent of others. My happiness depends on others' happiness. So when I see happy people, automatically I also feel a little bit happier than when I see people in a difficult situation. For example, when we see pictures on television which show people starving in Somalia, including old people and young children, then we automatically feel sad, regardless of whether that sadness can lead to some kind of active help or not.

Moreover, in our daily lives we are now utilizing many good facilities, including things like air-conditioned houses. All these things or facilities became possible, not because of ourselves, but because of many other people's direct or indirect involvement. Everything comes together. It is impossible to return to the way of life of a few centuries ago, when we depended on simple instruments, not all these machines. It is very clear to us that the facilities that we are enjoying now are the products of the activities of many people. In 24 hours you sleep on a bed – many people have been involved in that – and in the preparation of your food, too, especially for the non-vegetarian. Fame is definitely a product of other people – without the presence of other people the concept of fame would not even make sense. Also, the interest of Europe depends on America's interest and Western Europe's interest depends on the Eastern European economic situation. Each continent is heavily dependent on the others; that is the reality. Thus many of the things that we desire, such as wealth, fame and so forth, could not come into being without the active or indirect participation and co-operation of many other people.

Therefore, since we all have an equal right to be happy and since we are all linked to one another, no matter how important an individual is, logically the interest of the other five billion people on the planet is more important than that of one single person. By thinking along these lines, you can eventually develop a sense of global responsibility. Modern environmental problems, such as the depletion of the ozone layer, also clearly show us the need for world co-operation. It seems that with development, the whole world has become much smaller, but the human consciousness is still lagging behind.

This is not a question of religious practice, but a question of the future of humanity.

This kind of wider or more altruistic attitude is very relevant in today's world. If we look at the situation from various angles, such as the complexity and inter-connectedness of the nature of modern existence, then we will gradually notice a change in our outlook, so that when we say 'others' and when we think of others, we will no longer dismiss them as something that is irrelevant to us. We will no longer feel indifferent.

If you think only of yourself, if you forget the rights and well-being of others, or, worse still, if you exploit others, ultimately you will lose. You will have no friends who will show concern for your well-being. Moreover, if a tragedy befalls you, instead of feeling concerned, others might even secretly rejoice. By contrast, if an individual is compassionate and altruistic, and has the interests of others in mind, then irrespective of whether that person knows a lot of people, wherever that person moves, he or she will immediately make friends. And when that person faces a tragedy, there will be plenty of people who will come to help.

A true friendship develops on the basis of

genuine human affection, not money or power. Of course, due to your power or wealth, more people may approach you with big smiles or gifts. But deep down these are not real friends of yours; these are friends of your wealth or power. As long as your fortune remains, then these people will often approach you. But when your fortunes decline, they will no longer be there. With this type of friend, nobody will make a sincere effort to help you if you need it. That is the reality.

Genuine human friendship is on the basis of human affection, irrespective of your position. Therefore, the more you show concern about the welfare and rights of others, the more you are a genuine friend. The more you remain open and sincere, then ultimately more benefits will come to you. If you forget or do not bother about others, then eventually you will lose your own benefit. So sometimes I tell people, if we really are selfish, then wise selfishness is much better than the selfishness of ignorance and narrow-mindedness.

For Buddhist practitioners, the development of wisdom is also very important – and here I mean wisdom which realizes *Shunya*, the ultimate nature of reality. The realization of *Shunya* gives you at least some kind of positive sense about cessation. Once you have some kind of feeling for the possibility of cessation, then it becomes clear that suffering is not final and that there is an alternative. If there is alternative then it is worth making an effort. If only two of the Buddha's Four Noble Truths exist, suffering and the cause of suffering, then there is not much meaning. But the other two Noble Truths, including cessation, point towards an alternative way of existence. There is possibility of ending suffering. So it is worthwhile to realize the nature of suffering. Therefore wisdom is extremely important in increasing compassion infinitely.

So that is how one engages in the practice of Buddhism: there is an application of the faculty of wisdom, using intelligence, and an understanding of the nature of reality, together with the skilful means of generating compassion. I think that in your daily lives and in all sorts of your professional work, you can use this compassionate motivation.

Of course, in the field of education, there is no doubt that compassionate motivation is important and relevant. Irrespective of whether you are a believer or non-believer, compassion for the students' lives or futures, not only for their examinations, makes your work as a teacher much more effective. With that motivation, I think your students will remember you for the whole of their lives.

Similarly, in the field of health, there is an expression in Tibetan which says that the effectiveness of the treatment depends on how warm-hearted the physician is. Because of this expression, when treatments from a certain doctor do not work, people blame the doctor's character, speculating that perhaps that he or she was not a kind person. The poor doctor sometimes gets a very bad name! So in the medical field there is no doubt that compassionate motivation is something very relevant.

I think this is also the case with lawyers and politicians. If politicians and lawyers had more compassionate motivation then there would be less scandal. And as a result the whole community would get more peace. I think the work of politics would become more effective and more respected.

Finally, in my view, the worst thing is warfare. But even warfare with human affection and with human compassion is much less destructive. The completely mechanized warfare that is without human feeling is worse.

Also, I think compassion and a sense of responsibility can also enter into the fields of science and engineering. Of course, from a purely scientific point of view, awful weapons such as nuclear bombs are remarkable achievements. But we can say that these are negative because they bring immense suffering to the world. Therefore, if we do not take into account human pain, human feelings and human compassion, there is no demarcation between right and wrong. Therefore, human compassion can reach everywhere.

I find it a little bit difficult to apply this principle of compassion to the field of economics. But economists are human beings and of course they also need human affection, without which they would suffer. However, if you think only of profit, irrespective of the consequences, then drug dealers are not wrong, because, from the economic viewpoint, they are also making tremendous profits. But because this is very harmful for society and for the community, we call this wrong and name these people criminals. If that is the case, then I think arms dealers are in the same category. The arms trade is equally dangerous and irresponsible.

So I think for these reasons, human compassion, or what I sometimes call 'human affection', is the key factor for all human business. Just as you see that with the palm of our hand all five fingers become useful, if these fingers were not connected to the palm they would be useless. Similarly, every human action that is without human feeling becomes dangerous. With human feeling and an appreciation of human values, all human activities become constructive.

Even religion, which is supposedly good for humanity, without that basic human compassionate attitude can become foul. Unfortunately even now there are problems which are entirely down to different religions. So human compassion is something fundamental. If that is there, then all other human activities become more useful.

Generally speaking, I have the impression that in education and some other areas there is some negligence of the issue of human motivation. Perhaps in ancient times religion was supposed to carry this responsibility. But now in the community, religion generally seems a little bit old-fashioned, so people are losing interest in it and in deeper human values. However, I think these should be two separate things. If you have respect for or interest in religion, that is good. But even if you have no interest in religion, you should not forget the importance of these deeper human values.

There are various positive side-effects of enhancing one's feeling of compassion. One of them is that the greater the force of your compassion, the greater your resilience in confronting hardships and your ability to transform them into more positive conditions. One form of practice that seems to be quite effective is found in *A Guide to the Bodhisattva Way of Life*, a classic Buddhist text. In this practice you visualize your old self, the embodiment of self-centredness, self-ishness and so on, and then visualize a group of people who represent the masses of other sentient beings. Then you adopt a third person's point of view as a neutral, unbiased observer and make a comparative assessment of the value, the interests and then the importance of these two groups. Also try to reflect upon the faults of being totally oblivious to the well-being of other sentient beings and so on, and what this old self has really achieved as a result of leading such a way of life. Then reflect on the other sentient beings and see how important their well-being is, the need to serve them and so forth, and see what you, as a third neutral observer, would conclude as to whose interests and well-being are more important. You would naturally begin to feel more inclined towards the countless others.

I also think that the greater the force of your altruistic attitude towards sentient beings, the more courageous you become. The greater your courage, the less you feel prone to discouragement and loss of hope. Therefore, compassion is also a source of inner strength. With increased inner strength it is possible to develop firm determination and with determination there is a greater chance of success, no matter what obstacles there may be. On the other hand, if you feel hesitation, fear and a lack of self-confidence, then often you will develop a pessimistic attitude. I consider that to be the real seed of failure. With a pessimistic attitude you cannot accomplish even something you could easily achieve. Whereas even if something is difficult to achieve, if you have an unshakeable determination there is eventually the possibility of achievement. Therefore, even in the conventional sense, compassion is very important for a successful future.

As I pointed out earlier, depending on the level of your wisdom, there are different levels of compassion, such as compassion which is motivated by genuine insight into the ultimate nature of reality, compassion which is motivated by the appreciation of the impermanent nature of existence and compassion which is motivated by awareness of the suffering of other sentient beings. The level of your wisdom, or the depth of your insight into the nature of reality, determines the level of compassion that you will experience. From the Buddhist viewpoint, compassion with wisdom is very essential. It is as if compassion is like a very honest person and wisdom is like a very able person – if you join these two, then the result is something very effective.

I see compassion, love and forgiveness as common ground for all different religions, irrespective of tradition or philosophy. Although there are fundamental differences between different religious ideas, such as the acceptance of an Almighty Creator, every religion teaches us the same message: be a warm-hearted person. All of them emphasize the importance of compassion and forgiveness. Now in ancient times when the various religions were based in different places and there was less communication between them, there was no need for pluralism among the various religious traditions. But today, the world has become much smaller, so communication between different religious faiths has become very strong. Under such circumstances, I think pluralism among religious believers is very essential. Once you see the value to humanity through the centuries of these different religions through unbiased, objective study then there is plenty of reason to accept or to respect all these different religions. After all, in humanity there are so many different mental dispositions, so simply one religion, no matter how profound, cannot satisfy all the variety of people.

For instance, now, in spite of such a diversity of religious traditions, the majority of people still remain unattracted by religion. Of the five billion people, I believe only around one billion are true religious believers. While many people say, 'My family background is Christian, Muslim or Buddhist, so I'm a Christian, Muslim or Buddhist,' true believers, in their daily lives and particularly when some difficult situation arises, realize that they are followers of a particular religion. For example, I mean those who say, 'I am Christian,' and during that moment remember God, pray to God and do not let out negative emotions. Of these true believers, I think there are perhaps less than one billion. The rest of humanity, four billion people, remain in the true sense non-believers. So one religion obviously cannot satisfy all of humanity. Under such circumstances, a variety of religions is actually necessary and useful, and therefore the only sensible thing is that all different religions work together and live harmoniously, helping one another. There have been positive developments recently and I have noticed closer relations forming between various religions.

So, having reflected upon the faults of a self-centred way of thinking and life, and also having reflected upon the positive consequences of being mindful of the well-being of other sentient beings and working for their benefit, and being convinced of this, then in Buddhist meditation there is a special training which is known as 'the practice of Giving and Taking'. This is especially designed to enhance your power of compassion and love towards other sentient beings. It basically involves visualizing taking upon yourself all the suffering, pain, negativity and undesirable experiences of other sentient beings. You imagine taking these upon yourself and then giving away or sharing with others your own positive qualities, such as your virtuous states of mind, your positive energy, your wealth, your happiness and so forth. Such a form of training, though it cannot actually result in a reduction of suffering by other sentient beings or a production of your own positive qualities, psychologically brings about a transformation in your mind so effectively that your feeling of love and compassion is much more enhanced.

Trying to implement this practice in your daily life is quite powerful and can be a very positive influence on your mind and on your health. If you feel that it seems worthwhile to practise, then irrespective of whether you are a believer or a non-believer, you should try to promote these basic human good qualities.

One thing you should remember is that these mental transformations take time and are not easy. I think some people from the West, where technology is so good, think that everything is automatic. You should not expect this spiritual transformation to take place within a short period; that is impossible. Keep it in your mind and make a constant effort, then after 1 year, 5 years, 10 years, 15 years, you will eventually find some change. I still sometimes find it very difficult to practise these things. However, I really do believe that these practices are extremely useful.

My favourite quotation from Shantideva's book is: 'So long as sentient beings remain, so long as space remains, I will remain in order to serve, or in order to make some small contribution for the benefit of others.'

FIVE

INTERDEPENDENCE, INTER-CONNECTEDNESS AND THE NATURE OF REALITY

In a discussion of interdependence, inter-connectedness and the nature of reality, the first question is: what is time? We cannot identify time as some sort of independent entity. Generally speaking, there are external matters and internal feelings or experiences. If we look at the external things, then generally there is the past, the present and the future. Yet if we look closely at 'the present', such as the year, the month, the day, the hour, the minute, the second, we cannot find it. Just one second before the present is the past; and one second after is the future. There is no present. If there is no present, then it is difficult to talk about the past and the future, since both depend on the present. So if we look at external matters, it would seem that the past is just in our memory and the future is just in our imagination, nothing more than a vision.

But if we look at our internal experiences or states of consciousness, the past is no longer there and the future has not yet come: there is only the present. So things become somewhat complicated when we think along these lines. This is the nature of interdependency, the Sanskrit word *pratityasamutpada*. This is a very useful idea and it is one of my favourite subjects.

There are two levels of interdependency: a conventional level and a deeper level. First I will deal with the conventional level. When we speak of the Buddhist principle of interdependence, which is often referred to as 'interdependent origination', we must bear in mind that there are many different levels of understanding of that principle. The more superficial level of understanding of the principle is the interdependent nature or relationship between cause and effect. The deeper level of understanding of the principle is much more pervasive and, in fact, encompasses the entire spectrum of reality. The principle of interdependent origination in relation to cause and effect states that nothing can come about without the corresponding causes and conditions; everything comes into being as a result of an aggregation of causes and conditions.

If we consider the law of nature, we see it is not created by karma or by Buddha, it is just nature. We consider that Buddhahood developed according to natural law. Therefore, our experiences of pain and suffering, pleasure and joy, depend entirely on their own causes and conditions. Because of this natural relationship between causes and their effects, the Buddhist principle states that the greater your undesirability of a particular experience, event or phenomenon, the greater effort you must put into preventing the aggregation of its causes and conditions, so that you can prevent the occurrence of that event. And the greater your desirability of a particular event, outcome or experience, the greater attention you must pay to ensure that these causes and conditions are accumulated so that you can enjoy the outcome.

I personally believe that the relationship between a cause and an effect is also a sort of natural law. I don't think that one could come up with a rational explanation as to why effects necessarily follow concordant causes and conditions. For instance, it is stated that afflictive emotional states like anger and hatred lead to undesirable consequences, and according to the Buddhist scriptures, one consequence of hatred and anger is ugliness. But there is not a full, rational account as to *how* ugliness is a consequence of that particular afflictive emotion. Yet in a way one can understand it, because when you experience very intense anger or hatred, even your facial expression changes and you assume a very ugly face. Similarly, there are certain types of mental and cognitive emotional states which bring about almost instantaneous positive changes in your facial expression. These states bring you presence of mind, calmness and serenity and such an emotional state or thought could lead to a more desirable outcome. So one can see a type of connection, but not a full rational explanation.

But one might feel that there are certain types of emotional states, such as a very deep level of compassion, which are positive, yet, when they occur within your mind, one might say that at that particular instant there is no joy. For instance, a person may be fully under the influence of compassion and therefore sharing the suffering of the object of compassion. In that case, one could argue, from what I have said earlier, that compassion cannot be said to be a positive cause. But here I think one must understand that, while it is true that as a result of compassion, because one is fully engaged in sharing the suffering of the object of compassion, at that instant there is a certain degree of pain, this is very different from a pain which is being suffered by someone who is depressed, desperate and helpless and feels a loss of hope. In the case of compassionate suffering, although the person is undergoing a sort of pain, there is definitely a high degree of alertness, and there is no loss of control because the person is, in a way, willingly taking on the suffering of the other person. So on the surface these emotional states might look as though they have a similar outcome, but they are entirely different. In one case, the suffering is so overwhelming that the person has lost control and has given way to it, whereas in the case of compassion, the person is still in control of his or her thought.

Now if you understand the importance of appreciating the interdependent relationship between cause and effect, then you will appreciate the teachings on the Four Noble Truths. The entire teaching on the Four Noble Truths is based on the principle of causality. When the causal principle that is implied in these teachings is elaborated, you read Buddha's doctrine of the Twelve Links of Dependent Origination. In that teaching he stated that, because there is a particular cause, its effects follow; because the cause was created, the effect came about; and because there was ignorance, it led to action or karma.

So here you find three statements: one is that because the cause exists, the effect follows; because the cause was created, the effect was produced; and because there was ignorance, it led to the action. Now the first statement indicates that, from an affirmative point of view, when causes are aggregated, effects will naturally follow. And what is also implied in that statement is that it is due to the mere aggregation of the causes and conditions that the effects come into being, and that, apart from the causal process, there is no external power or force such as a Creator and so forth which brings these things into being.

The second statement again points out another important characteristic of dependent origination, which is that the very cause which brings about the effects must itself have a cause. If the cause is an eternally existing, permanent absolute entity, then such an entity could not be itself an effect of something else. If that is the case, then it will not have the potential to produce an effect. Therefore, first of all there must be a cause; second, that very cause must itself have a cause.

And the third statement points out another important characteristic of the principle of dependent origination. It is that the effect must be commensurate with the cause – there must be a concordance between the two. Not just anything can produce anything; there must be a sort of special relatioship between cause and effect. Buddha gave an example of ignorance leading to action. Here the implication is, 'Who commits that action?' It is a sentient being – and by committing an act motivated by an ignorant state of mind that being is in a way accumulating his or her own downfall. Since there is no living being that desires unhappiness or suffering, it is due to ignorance that the individual engages in an act which has the potential to produce undesirable consequences.

So we find that the entire Twelve Links of Dependent Origination fall into three classes of phenomena. First, there are afflictive emotions and thoughts; second, there is the karmic action and its imprints; and third, there is its effect: suffering. So the principal message is that suffering is something that we all do not desire, but it is a consequence or an effect of ignorance. Buddha did not state that suffering is an effect of consciousness, because if that was the case, then the process of liberation or the process of purification would necessarily involve putting an end to the very continuum of consciousness. One moral that we can draw from this teaching is that the sufferings which are rooted in afflictive and negative emotions and thoughts can be removed. This ignorant state of mind can be dispelled, because we can generate insight which perceives the nature of reality. So we see that the principle of dependent origination shows how all these 12 links in the chain of dependent origination which forms an individual's entry into the cycle of existence are inter-connected.

Now if we were to apply this inter-connectedness to our perception of reality as a whole, then we could generate a great insight from it. For instance, we would then be able to appreciate the interdependent nature of one's own and others' interests: how the interests and well-being of human beings is dependent upon the well-being of animals living on the same planet. Similarly, if we develop such an understanding of the nature of reality, we would also be able to appreciate the inter-connectedness between the well-being of human beings and the natural environment. We could also consider the present, the future and so forth. We would then be able to cultivate an outlook on reality which is very holistic and has very significant implications.

So in a few words, you can see that there are no independent causes of one's own happiness. It depends on many other factors. So the conclusion is that in order to have a happier future for oneself, you have to take care of everything which relates to you. That is, I think, quite a useful view.

So far, I have spoken about the principle of dependent origination from the perspective of the first level of understanding. We can see in the Buddhist scriptures the importance of understanding this level of the dependent origination. In fact, one of the Mahayana texts known as *Compendium of Deeds*, in which Shantideva quotes heavily from Buddha's *sutras*, points out the need to first of all appreciate the inter-connectedness of all events and phenomena: how, due to the causal and conditional process, phenomena and events come into being; and how crucial it is to respect that conventional reality, because it is at that level that we can understand how certain types of experiences lead to certain types of undesirable consequences, how certain causes, certain types of aggregation of causes and conditions can lead to more desirable consequences, and so forth; how, in fact, certain events can directly affect our well-being and experience. Because there is that sort of relation, it is very crucial for practising Buddhists to first develop a deep understanding of the perspective of the first level. Then Buddha states that one should go beyond that understanding and question the ultimate nature of the things that relate to each other in this inter-connected way. This points towards the Buddha's teachings on Emptiness.

In the teachings on the Twelve Links of Dependent Origination, the Buddha states that, although sentient beings do not desire suffering and dissatisfaction, it is through ignorance that they accumulate karmic actions which then lead to undesirable consequences. Now the question then is: what exactly is the nature of that ignorance? What is the mechanism that really leads an individual to act against what he or she fundamentally desires? Here Buddha points to the role of afflictive emotions and thoughts, like anger, hatred, attachment and so forth, which blind the person's understanding of the nature of reality. If we were to examine the state of mind at the point when an individual experiences an intense emotion like hatred, anger or extreme attachment, we would find that, at that point, the person has a rather false notion of self: there is a kind of unquestioned assumption of an independently existing 'I' or subject or person which is perceived, not necessarily consciously, as a kind of a master. It is not totally independent from the body or mind, nor is it to be identified with the body or mind, but there is something there which is somehow identified as the core of the being, the self, and there is a strong sort of grasping at that kind of identity or being. Based on that, you have strong emotional experiences, like attachment towards loved ones, or strong anger or hatred towards someone whom you perceive as threatening, and so forth.

Similarly, if we were to examine how we really perceive our object of desire or object of anger, we would notice that there is a kind of assumption of an independently existing entity, something which is worthy of being desired or worthy of being hated. Aside from the subtle perspective of the doctrine of

Emptiness, even in our day-to-day lives we often find a disparity between the way we perceive things and the way things really exist. If that was not true, then the very idea of being deceived would not make sense. We often find ourselves totally disillusioned because we had false perceptions of reality. Once our illusion is dispelled, we realize that we have been deceived. So we often see in our own daily life cases where the appearance of something does not tally with the reality of the situation.

Similarly, as I pointed out in my talk on subtle impermanence, even from the perspective of the transient nature of phenomena there is often a big disparity between the way in which we perceive things and the way things really are. For instance, when we meet someone we say, 'Oh, this is the very same person I've known for a long time.' Again, when you see an object, you think, 'Oh, this is the same object which I saw two days ago.' This is a very crude way of talking about reality. What is actually happening here is a kind of a conflation between an image or a concept of an entity and the actual reality of the moment. In reality, the object or entity that we are perceiving has already gone through a lot of stages. It is dynamic, it is transient, it is momentary, so the object that we are perceiving now is never the same as the one which we perceived a day ago or two days ago, but we have the impression that we are perceiving the very same one because what we are doing is conflating the concept of that object and the actual object. So we see again here a disparity between the way things appear to us and the way in which things really exist. Similarly, if we were to take the perspective of modern physics, then we would also find that there is a disparity between the common-sense view of reality and how scientists, from their point of view, would explain the nature of reality.

So what is clear from all this is the fact that there is some fault in our identification of an individual being as a self, as a person or as an individual. But the question is: to what extent is it false? We cannot accept that the self or 'I' does not exist at all, because if that is the case then a lot of our concerns, projects and actions would not make any sense.

Because of the fact that there is a self, our concerns for attaining full liberation for the sake of other sentient beings, our concern for the well-being of other sentient beings, becomes very serious, because there is someone or something who would either suffer or benefit as a result of the stand we adopt or actions we engage in. So the question really is: to what extent is our notion of self, our sense of identity, our understanding of the being or individual, false or deceived, and to what extent is it correct? Making the demarcation between the correct view of the self and person and the false view of the self and person is extremely difficult. It is because of this difficulty – yet at the same time the importance of being able to make such a distinction – that there emerged in India various Buddhist philosophical schools. Some schools only accept 'identitylessness' of persons, but not of external events or phenomena; some schools accept the 'identitylessness' of not only persons but also of entire existence, and even within that school there are various subtleties.

The reason why so much importance is

placed on making the distinction is because it is so crucial to our attempt to liberate ourselves from suffering and its causes. This in part answers one of the questions that arose in one of the previous talks, that, if Buddhism accepts the doctrine of 'no-self', what is it that takes rebirth?

We know that the doctrine of no-self or *anatman* is common to all the Buddhist schools of thought. The common doctrine of no-self is understood in terms of the denial of an independent and permanent self or soul. But what I will be presenting here is the understanding of Nagarjuna, as interpreted by the Indian pandit Chandrakirti. Nagarjuna, in his principal philosophical work, *The Fundamental Treatise on the Middle Way*, states that it is ignorance or misapprehension of the nature of reality which is at the root of our suffering. The manner in which one can attain liberation from suffering is by dispelling this ignorant state of mind, this misconceived notion of reality, by generating insight into the ultimate nature of reality. Nagarjuna identifies two types of ignorance: one is grasping at an inherent or intrinsic reality of one's own self or being; the other is grasping at an inherent and independent existence of external events and things. He goes on to state that this grasping at a 'self' or 'I' comes about as a result of grasping at our aggregates: our body, mind and mental functions. He further states that the fact that we have to dispel this ignorance from within our minds, that we have to see through the misconception of our misapprehension, is clear. But simply by distancing ourselves from that grasping, simply by thinking that it is false, simply by thinking that it is destructive and so on cannot ultimately help to free the individual from such forms of grasping. It is only by seeing through the illusion of that apprehension, it is only by generating an insight that would directly contradict the way in which, through that ignorance, we would normally perceive reality that we will be able to dispel that ignorance.

So how do we go about seeing through the illusion of this false notion of self? How do we generate the insight that would directly contradict that form of perception? Nagarjuna says that if a 'self', 'I' or person exists as we normally assume it to exist, if it exists as we falsely view it, then the more we look for it, the more we search for its essence, the referent behind our terms and labels, then the clearer it should become. But that is not the case. If we were to search for the self or person as we normally perceive it, then it disappears, it sort of disintegrates, and this is an indication that such a notion of self was an illusion from the start. Because of this point, one of Nagarjuna's students, Aryadeva, stated in his *Four Hundred Verses on the Middle Way* that it is our ignorant conception or consciousness which is the seed of *samsara* (cyclic existence) and that things and events are its objects of grasping and apprehension. And it is only by seeing through the illusion of such a conception that we will be able to put an end to the process of existence.

We find in Nagarjuna's own writings extensive reasoning to refute the validity of our notion of self and negate the existence of self or person as we falsely perceive it. He argues that if the self or person is identical with the body, then just as the body is momentary, transient, changing every day, the self or the person should also be subject to the same law. For instance, a human being's bodily continuity can cease and, if the self is identical with the body, then the continuum of the self will also cease at that point. On the other hand, if the self is totally independent of the body, then how can it make sense to say, when a person is physically ill, that the *person* is ill, and so forth? Therefore, apart from the interrelationships between various factors that form our being, there is no independent self.

Similarly, if we extend the same analysis to external reality, we find that, for example, every material object has directional parts, certain parts facing towards different directions. We know that so long as it is an entity it is composed of parts and that there is a kind of necessary relationship between the whole and its parts, so we find that apart from the interrelationship between the various parts and the idea of wholeness, there is no independent entity existing outside that interface. We can apply the same analysis to consciousness or mental phenomena. Here the only difference is that the characteristics of consciousness or mental phenomena are not material or physical. However, we can analyse this in terms of the various instants or moments that form a continuum.

Since we cannot find the essence behind the label, or since we cannot find the referent behind the term, does it mean that nothing exists? The question could also be raised: is that absence of phenomena the meaning of the doctrine of Emptiness? Nagarjuna anticipates the criticism from the realists' perspective which argues that if phenomena do not exist as we perceive them, if phenomena cannot be found when we search for their essence, then they do not exist. Therefore, a person or self would not exist. And if a person does not exist, then there is no action or karma because the very idea of karma involves someone committing the act; and if there is no karma, then there cannot be suffering because there is no experiencer, then there is no cause. And if that is the case, there is no possibility of freedom from suffering because there is nothing from which to be freed. Furthermore, there is no path that would lead to that freedom. And if that is the case, there cannot be a spiritual community or *sangha* that would embark on the path towards that liberation. And if that is the case, then there is no possibility of a fully perfected being or Buddha. So the realists argue that if Nagarjuna's thesis is true, that the essence of things cannot be found, then nothing will exist and one will have to deny the existence of *samsara* and Nirvana and everything.

Nagarjuna says that such a criticism, that these consequences would follow from his thesis, indicates a lack of understanding of the subtle meaning of the doctrine of Emptiness, because the doctrine of Emptiness does not state or imply the non-existence of everything. Also the doctrine of Emptiness is not simply the thesis that things cannot be found when searched for their essence. The meaning of Emptiness is the interdependent nature of reality.

Nagarjuna goes on to say what he means by the claim that the true meaning of Emptiness emerges from an understanding of the principle of dependent origination. He states that because phenomena are dependent originations, because phenomena come about as a result of interdependent relationships between causes and conditions, they are empty. They are empty of inherent and independent status. An appreciation of that view is understanding of the true Middle Way. In other words, when we understand dependent origination, we see that not only the existence of phenomena, but also the identity of phenomena, depend upon other factors.

So dependent origination can dispel extremes of both absolutism and nihilism, because the idea of 'dependence' points towards a form of existence which lacks independent or absolute status, therefore it liberates the individual from extremes of absolutism. In addition, 'origination' frees the individual from falling to the extremes of nihilism, because origination points towards an understanding of existence, that things do exist.

I stated earlier that the unfindability of phenomena or entities when we search for their essence is not really a full meaning of Emptiness, but at the same time it indicates that phenomena lack intrinsic reality, they lack independent and inherent existence. What is meant by this is that their existence and their identity are derived from mere interaction of various factors. Buddhapalita, one of the disciples of Nagarjuna, states that because phenomena come about due to interaction of various factors, their very existence and identity are derived from other factors. Otherwise, if they had independent existence, if they possessed intrinsic reality, then there would be no need for them to be dependent on other factors. The very fact that they depend on other factors is an indication that they lack independent or absolute status.

So the full understanding of Emptiness can come about only when one appreciates the subtlety of this principle of dependent origination – if one concludes that the ultimate nature is that phenomena cannot be found if we were to search for their essence. Nagarjuna states that if the principle or doctrine of Emptiness is not valid, if phenomena are not devoid of independent and inherent existence and intrinsic reality, then they will be absolute; therefore there will be no room for the principle of dependent origination to operate and there will be no room for the interdependent principle to operate. If that is the case, it would not be possible for causal principles to operate and therefore the holistic perception of reality also becomes a false notion. And if that is so, then the whole idea of the Four Noble Truths will be invalid because there is no causal principle operating. Then you will be denying the entire teachings of the Buddha.

In fact, what Nagarjuna does is to reverse all the criticisms levelled against his thesis, by stating that in the realists' position all the teachings of the Buddha would have to be denied. He sums up his criticism by saying that any system of belief or practice which denies the doctrine of Emptiness can explain nothing coherently, whereas any system of belief or thought which accepts this principle of interdependent origination, this doctrine of Emptiness, can come up with a coherent account of reality.

So what we find here is a very interesting complementary relationship between the two levels of understanding of dependent origination I spoke of earlier. The perspective of the first level really accounts for much of our everyday existence or everyday world of experience, where causes and conditions interact and there is a causal principle operating. That perspective of dependent origination, according to Buddhism, is called the correct view at the worldly level. The greater your appreciation of that perspective, the closer you will be able to come to the deeper level of understanding of dependent origination, because your understanding of the causal mechanism at that level is used to arrive at an understanding of the empty nature of all phenomena. Similarly, once your insight into the empty nature of all phenomena becomes deep, then your conviction in the efficacy of causes and effects will be strengthened, so there will be a greater respect for the conventional reality and relative world. So there is a kind of interesting complementary relationship between the two perspectives.

As your insight into the ultimate nature of reality and Emptiness is deepened and enhanced, you will develop a perception of reality from which you will perceive phenomena and events as sort of illusory, illusion-like, and this mode of perceiving reality will permeate all your interactions with reality. Consequently, when you come across a situation in which you generate compassion, instead of becoming more detached from the object of compassion, your engagement will be deeper and fuller. This is because compassion is ultimately founded upon a valid mode of thought and you will have gained a deeper insight into the nature of reality. Conversely, when you confront situations which would normally give rise to afflictive, negative emotions and responses on your part, there will be a certain degree of detachment and you will not fall prey to the influences of those negative and afflictive emotions. This is because, underlying those afflictive emotions and thoughts, such as desire, hatred, anger and so forth, there is a mistaken notion of reality, which involves grasping at things as absolute, independent and unitary. When you generate insight into Emptiness, the grip of these emotions on your mind will be loosened.

At the beginning of my talk I gave an

example of our concept of time: ordinarily we presume there is a kind of an independent existent or independent entity called 'time' present or past or future. But when we examine it at a deeper level, we find it is a mere convention. Other than the interface between the three tenses, the present, future and past, there is no such thing as an independently existing present moment, so we generate a sort of dynamic view of reality. Similarly, when I think of myself, although initially I might have an unquestioned assumption of there being an independent self, when I look closer I will find that, apart from the interface of various factors that constitute my being and various moments of the continuum that form my being, there is no such thing as an absolute independent entity. Since it is this mere conventional 'self', 'I' or person that goes towards the attainment of liberation or eventually transforms into Buddha, even Buddha is not absolute.

There is a similar case with the phenomenon mentioned earlier, the idea of Clear Light, which is the most subtle level of consciousness. Again, one should not conceive of it as some kind of independently existing entity. Apart from the continuum of consciousness which forms this phenomenon called Clear Light, we cannot speak of an independently existing absolute entity.

Likewise, we will find that many of our concepts indicate a very deep, very complex inter-connectedness. For instance, when we speak of ourselves as subjects, we can make sense of that notion only in relation to an object – the idea of a subject makes sense only in relation to an object. Similarly, the idea of action makes sense in relation to a being, an agent who commits the act. So if we were to analyse a lot of these concepts, we would find we cannot really separate the entity or the phenomenon from its context.

Again, if we go beyond the idea that things are mere designations or labels and ask whose conceptual thought creates the labels, whether it is the past conception or the future conception, whether it is the conception of a particular being or the collective conception, and so forth, we will not find an independent existence.

Even Emptiness itself, which is seen as the

ultimate nature of reality, is not absolute, nor does it exist independently. We cannot conceive of Emptiness as independent of a basis of phenomena, because when we examine the nature of reality we find that it is empty of inherent existence. Then if we are to take that Emptiness itself as an object and look for its essence or its status of existence, again we will find that it is empty of inherent existence. Therefore Buddha taught the Emptiness of Emptiness. However, when we search for the true essence of a phenomenon or event, what we find is this Emptiness. But that does not mean that Emptiness itself is absolute, because Emptiness as a concept or as an entity cannot withstand this analysis. If we were to take Emptiness itself as an object and then again examine it, we cannot find it. However in some scriptures we will find references to Emptiness as ultimate truth. Here one should understand what is the meaning of this term 'ultimate'. One should not mistake it in terms of Emptiness as being ultimately true, or it being absolute, but rather it is called 'ultimate truth' because it is an object of the insight that has penetrated into the nature of reality.

history, I am quite sure that many aspects of their religious teachings and traditions reflect the needs and concerns of different times and cultures. Therefore, I think it is quite important to be able to make a distinction between what I call the 'core' and 'essence' of religious teachings and the cultural aspects of the particular tradition. What I would call the 'essence' or 'core' of religious traditions are the basic religious messages, such as the principles of love, compassion and so forth, which always retain their relevance and importance, irrespective of time and circumstances. But as time changes, the cultural context changes, and I think it is important for the followers of religious traditions to be able to make the necessary changes that would reflect the particular concerns of their time and culture.

I think the most important task of any religious practitioner is to examine oneself within one's own mind and try to transform one's body, speech and mind, and act according to the teachings and the principles of the religious tradition that one is following. This is very important. Conversely, if one's faith or practice of religion remains only at the intellectual level of knowledge, such as being familiar with certain doctrines without translating them into one's behaviour or conduct, then I think that is a grave mistake. In fact, if someone possesses certain intellectual knowledge of religious traditions or teachings, yet his or her consciousness and mental continuum remain totally uninfluenced by it, then this could be quite destructive. It could lead to a situation in which the person, because of having the knowledge of the religious beliefs, could use the religion for the purposes of exploitation and manipulation. So, I think, as practitioners, our first responsibility is to watch ourselves.

The situation of today's world is completely different from the past. In the past, human communities and societies remained more or less independent of one another. Under such circumstances, ideas of a single religion, a monolithic culture and so forth, made sense and had a place in the cultural context. But this situation has now completely changed as a result of various factors: easy access between various countries, an information revolution, easy transportation, and so forth. So human society can no longer function on that model.

Let us take as an example the city of London. London is a city which is multi-cultural and has multiple religions. There-fore, if we don't exercise caution and utilize our intelligence, there is a possibility of con-flict based on divergent religious beliefs and cultures. So it is very important to have an outlook that takes into account the existence of multiple religions, the plurality of reli-gions. The best way to meet this challenge is not just to study other religious traditions through reading books, but more importantly to meet with people from other religious tra-ditions so that you can share experiences with them and learn from their experiences. Through personal contact you will be able to really appreciate the value of other religious traditions.

From a wider perspective, there are defi-nitely strong grounds for appreciating plur-alism in religion and culture, particularly in religion. It is a fact that among humanity there are many diverse mental dispositions, interests, needs and so on. Therefore, the greater the diversity of religious traditions that are available, the greater their capacity to meet the needs of different people.

In the history of humanity there have been very tragic events which came about because of religion. Even to this day, we see that conflicts arise in the name of religion and the human community is further divided. If we were to meet this challenge, then I am sure we would find that there are enough grounds on which we can build harmony between the various religions and develop a genuine respect towards each other.

Another important challenge facing humanity now is the issue of environmental protection. In fact, a number of prominent environmentalists have expressed their wish to see more active initiatives taken by the different religious traditions and especially by their leaders. I think this is a wish that is very valid. Personally, I feel that much of the environmental problem really stems from our insatiable desire, lack of contentment and greed. It is in the religious teachings that we find various instructions that enable us to keep a check on our desires and greed, and to positively transform our behaviour and conduct. Therefore, I think religious traditions have not only a potential but also a great responsibility to make contributions in that direction.

Another thing that I consider very important, and which is a responsibility that religious traditions must take upon themselves, is the putting forward of a united front against war and conflict. I know that in human history there have been a few cases where, through war, freedom has been won and certain goals have been achieved. But I personally believe that war cannot ever lead to the ultimate solution of a problem. Therefore, I think it is important for all the religious traditions to take a united stand and voice their opposition to the very idea of war. But voicing one's opposition to war alone is not enough. We must do something to bring about an end to war and conflict, and one of the things that we have to seriously think about is the question of disarmament. I know that the motivating factor which triggers the need for weapons is human emotion – hatred and anger. But there is no way that we can completely eliminate anger and hatred from the minds of human beings. We can definitely reduce their force and alleviate them, but not completely eliminate them. That means that we have to make serious efforts to achieve disarmament.

Another challenge that we face is the question of population. I know that from the point of view of all religious traditions, life, human life in particular, is precious. From the viewpoint of individual human beings, the more humans there are the better it is, because then we have the opportunity for more human lives to come into being. However, if we look at this issue from a global perspective, then I think there is definitely a need for all religious traditions to give the population issue very serious thought, because the world's resources are limited. There is only a certain degree to which world resources can sustain human beings on this planet.

SEVEN

QUESTIONS
AND ANSWERS
On Various Problems of the Modern Age

Q: On pollution and on the end of the universe
Your Holiness, what is your answer on how to stop pollution in the universe? Will there have to be an end of the universe and mankind as we know them in order to cleanse and begin again?

A: *Of course, from the Buddhist viewpoint, not just from that of common sense, there is a beginning and there is an end. That is logical; that is law; that is nature. So whatever we call the Big Bang or such things, there is a process of evolution or a process of beginning. So there must be an end. In any case, I think the end won't come for several million years.*

Now, pollution. As you know I come

from Tibet. When we were in Tibet, we had no idea about pollution. Things were very clean! In fact, when I first came across pollution and heard people say that I could not drink the water, it was a surprise to me. Eventually our knowledge widened.

Now it is really a very serious issue. It is not a question of one nation or two nations, but of the survival and health of all of humanity. If we have a clear conscience about this problem and behave accordingly, it seems there is a way to at least lessen this problem. For example, two or three years ago when I was in Stockholm beside the big river, some of my friends told me that 10 years previously there had been no fish in the river because the water was so polluted. Around the time of my visit some fish had begun to appear because of the control of pollution. So this shows that there is the possibility of improving things.

Killing and situations like Bosnia are immediately striking to our minds. Yet *pollution and other environmental problems lack this kind of striking appearance. Gradually, month by month, year by year, things become worse and worse. By the time a problem becomes very obvious it may be too late. Therefore I think it is a very serious matter. I am quite encouraged that in many places people are clearly concerned, and even some political parties have been set up based on the ideology and policy of environmental protection. I think this is a very healthy development. So there is hope.*

Q: On human suffering
Your Holiness, in this modern world, we try to avoid suffering. This only seems to create more suffering in that one person's positive work can be someone else's suffering, for instance medicine, politics and so on. How do we judge? Shouldn't we just accept a certain amount of suffering and discomfort?

A: *I think that there are many levels of suffering. Generally speaking, it is definitely possible to reduce the level of suffering. I don't personally believe that conditions that are essential for one's well-being and happiness necessarily involve harming and affecting someone else's life in a negative way.*

Here I would like to say something. I feel that television and newspapers usually report negative things. Killings, for example, or unfortunate events are immediately reported. In the meantime, millions of people are actually receiving help, or being nourished or looked after by human affection, such as millions of children, sick and old people. But usually in people's minds these good things are taken for granted. They are not seen as something to which we should pay special attention. Actually, this shows that the very nature of humanity is compassion or affection. We simply ignore all the work of affection because it seems natural. But we are surprised at things like bloodshed; it shocks our minds because our nature is not of that kind. As a result, many people get the impression that human nature is negative, aggressive and violent. I think that psychologically this is very bad, especially for young children who, through television, see negative human elements, but always for a short time. At that moment or for a short period, these things like killing or hitting can be a little bit exciting. But in the long-term, I think these violent things are very, very harmful to society. In fact, I recently had a meeting with Karl Popper, the philosopher. We have known each other since my first visit to this country in 1973. In our meeting we discussed violence on television and my view that too much violence is having a very negative impact on the minds of millions of children. He is, I think, of the same opinion. A proper way of education is the most important element in terms of hope for a better future.

Q: On racism, bigotry and human folly
Your Holiness, racism, bigotry and human folly seem to be on the increase. To what negative factors do you ascribe this? What positive factors can combat this trend?

A: *I think they largely depend on education. I feel that the more correct information and the more awareness and contact you have, the better. Of course, you also have to adopt an open mind. After all, you are just one human being out of five billion and one individual's future depends very much on others. Part of the problem I see is a lack of awareness of other cultures and the existence of other communities, and also a lack of understanding of the nature or reality of modern existence. If it were possible to gain complete satisfaction and fulfilment by being totally independent within one's own culture and one's own community – to be totally independent and unrelated to other communities around the world – then perhaps one could argue that there were* grounds for subscribing to these misconceptions like bigotry and racism. But this is not the case. The reality of the existence of other cultures and other communities cannot be ignored. Moreover, the nature of modern existence is such that the well-being, happiness and success of one's own community are very connected with the well-being and interests of other communities and other societies. In such a complex modern world there is no room for bigotry and racism.

Now according to my own experience, there is no doubt that Buddhism is the most suitable religion for me. But this does not mean that Buddhism is best for everyone. Each individual has a different mental disposition and therefore for some people a particular religion is more suitable or more effective than others. So if I respect each individual's right, then I must respect or accept the value of these different religions because they work for millions of other people.

When I was in Tibet I had little information, through books or from personal *contact, about the nature and value of other traditions. Since I've become a refugee, I have had more opportunity to have closer contact with other traditions, mainly through individuals, and I have gained a much deeper understanding of their value. As a result, my attitude now is that each one is a valid religion. Of course, even from the philosophical viewpoint, I still believe that Buddhist philosophy is more sophisticated, that it has more variety or is more vast, but all other religions still have tremendous benefits or great potential. So on both bases, I think my attitude towards other religions is greatly changed. Today, wherever I go and whenever I meet someone who follows a different religion, I deeply admire their practice and I very sincerely respect their tradition.*

Q: On bringing up children
What are the most important features in bringing up young children?

A: *I think you should ask a specialist. That would be better!*

Q: On money
How can one live well in a society based around the need to earn money?

A: *I think there is the possibility of balancing that with living well. For instance, even Tibetans need to earn money. Especially me at this moment with the exiled government – I think our deficit this year is over two million dollars! So I am very, very worried about that!*

Q: On birth control and the population explosion
Your Holiness, do you have any recommendations about the population explosion in the world?

A: *I think there is no doubt that birth control is necessary. Abortion is very, very sad. However, I think contraception is very necessary. Sometimes I jokingly tell people that it would be best if there were more nuns and monks. Isn't that the best non-violent method of population control?!*

Q: On religion in the modern world
Your Holiness, in this country there has been a move away from religion in recent years. At the same time, there has been an increased interest in various forms of self-development. Is religion still an appropriate path in the modern world?

A: *It is definitely relevant in the modern world. But perhaps I should clarify this. Many years have passed since various religious traditions started, so certain aspects are, I think, perhaps out of date. But this does not mean that religion as a whole is irrelevant in modern times. Therefore, it is important to look at the essence of the different religions, including Buddhism. Human beings, no matter whether today's or those of 100, 1,000, 4,000 or 5,000 years ago, are basically the same. Of course, a lot of the cultures and the ways of life have changed, but still we have the same kind of human being. So therefore, the basic human problems and suffering – such as death, old age, disease, fighting and all these things – are still there. I don't know what kind of shape humans will be in after 10,000 years or 100,000 years; nobody knows. But at least over the last few thousand years, they have, I think, kept basically the same nature.*

So I think the various different religions actually deal with basic human suffering and problems. On that level, because human nature and suffering have remained the same, the religions are still very relevant. On the other hand, certain ceremonial aspects and so on have changed. In India, during the feudal system or the reign of kings, the way of practice was very much influenced by those circumstances. But that has changed and, I think, has to change further.

As far as Buddhism is concerned, it of course not only deals with this life but with other more mysterious aspects.

Unless, just as modernization is taking place in our world, a similar type of modernization is taking place in other realms of existence, I think Buddhism will retain its relevance and appropriateness, not only to our modern world, because many of the fundamental problems of human existence still remain, but also because it addresses issues which are related to other mysterious forms of existence. I always believe that the modern change is just a surface change and that deep down we are the same. Last year at the border between Austria and Italy, they recovered an old body. If we were to suppose that the person was alive, I think we could still communicate with him. Yet the body is about 4,000 years old. Of course, that person would have a different culture and maybe a slightly different way of expression, but basically we could still communicate.

Q: On retribution and the situation in Bosnia

You said that without hatred, retribution

may be positive in order to prevent another from committing misdeeds. Would Your Holiness make any comment on the advisability of the United Nations authorizing air strikes against the Bosnian Serbs?

A: *Oh, that's really too complicated! The only thing we can do is simply share their misery and suffering. It's a very sad situation. Other than sharing their misery in our minds, there doesn't seem to be much we can really do. To me, all of these problems and chaotic situations in Bosnia, as well as in the former Soviet republics and in Africa, do not just come about suddenly. The causes of these developments run through decades. Therefore, we should learn from these events. In future, I think that if there is an area where there is the potential for this kind of crisis, the world community must pay full attention to it right from the beginning and take appropriate measures. I think this is very necessary.*

Regarding human rights violations,

now it is very encouraging that people all over the world have a new outlook regarding human rights issues. This is very healthy and good. But I consider human rights violations and similar sorts of problems also as symptoms. For instance, if there is some swelling or pimple on the surface of the skin, it is because something is wrong in the body. It is not sufficient to just treat the symptoms – you must look deeper and try to find the main cause. You should try to change the fundamental causes, so that the symptoms automatically disappear.

Similarly, I think that there is something wrong with our basic structure, especially in the field of international relations. I often tell my friends in the United States and here: 'You cherish democracy and freedom very much. Yet when you deal with foreign countries, nobody follows the principle of democracy, but rather you look to economic power or military force. Very often in international relations, people are more concerned with force or strength than with democratic principles.' I think I can go further: the highest international body, the United Nations itself, which was founded because of the situation just after World World II, has, for example, five nations with permanent seats in the Security Council, each with the power of veto. This is not democratic. Moreover, in Africa, where millions die from starvation, weapons are available but food is not. This area has real opportunities, but millions of dollars are spent on buying weapons! I think it's very sad.

So, as we have discussed, hatred is our enemy and weapons are also our enemy. Of course, when I was young I thought that weapons, air rifles, for example, were very beautiful. I loved to polish them! But the real purpose of these weapons is killing! Awful. We must do something about these beautiful but awful weapons.

And as for the military establishment... I think in the Western tradition, it is common for the son of the King or

Queen to be sent to a military academy or into the navy. People feel proud of this. But I will tell you one small story. Last year, a German television team came to see me and one of the things they said was that, while Westerners are very, very afraid of death, Easterners do not seem afraid of death. I jokingly told them that the exact opposite was the case. You are so fond of military things. Not only do you yourselves build military forces, but you also sell arms. Arms and the military establishment are intended to kill. But in the East, even if one insect is killed there is a sense of repentance. For example, once, when I was in Tibet, a person was murdered and everyone was shocked. It was something really unbelievable. So it seems that Westerners are not afraid of death, while Easterners really fear death. I really feel that. So I think that mentally there's something wrong with the concept of war and the military establishment. One way or another, we must make every attempt to reduce the military forces.

Anyway, with regard to the Bosnians and particularly your question about Bosnia, I have no clear answer – no idea.

Q: On overcoming the negativity of the news and media
What suggestions can you offer to overcome social institutions, such as the news, entertainment and media, which seem constantly to promote negative attitudes and emotions – the opposite of what you advocate?

A: *That is true. I often express my concern at that. However, I think as we discussed, much depends on our own mental attitude. When we look at these negative things – killing, sex or that kind of thing – if we look at them from another angle, that is also useful. Sometimes you can use these scenes of violence, sex and so forth in a more positive way, so that, by being mindful of the effect and destructive nature of these various human emotions, you can use this particular viewing as a reminder of*

135

their destructive nature. While images of sex and violence may be somewhat exciting initially, if you look further you can see no benefit.

Of course, I have another opinion of the media, I think especially in the West. In a country like India, killing and murder is often shown on television, but the sexual things are more censored. But if you compare killing and sex, sex is much better! If we pretend that it is not a part of human life, that is also not good, is it?

Anyway, I think it is equally important to make a clear presentation to the human mind of the other, good, human qualities, and I think that this is lacking. We only show the negative side – killing, sex and all these things – but the other side, the human acts of compassion, are not shown.

Now, for example, about 10 days ago in Washington I visited the museum of the Holocaust. When I went there, after seeing all these things, I was reminded of both qualities of human beings. On the one side there was Nazi Germany's torture, killing and extermination of the Jewish people – horrible and very sad. It reminds me how bad or awful it is if human intelligence is guided or motivated by hatred. But at the same time, another side showed those people who sacrificed their own lives in order to protect Jewish people. So that also shows the human good quality, to risk even their own lives to save unfortunate people. In that way, I think it was quite balanced. If we let hatred guide us then we can be so cruel and so destructive. But on the other hand, if we promote good human qualities, then wonderful actions and marvellous things can happen. Likewise, the media should show both sides. That is what I always feel.

Q: On genetic engineering
Scientists and doctors can now help people choose the sex of their baby. What does Your Holiness think about genetic engineering and what effect does it have

on the unborn? Should the unborn have the choice, or the parents?

A: *I think it's very difficult to give a general answer to this. I think we have to study it case by case. Of course, in some cases such work may be positive; so that's difficult.*

Q: On the world's political leaders
Do you think that the world's political leaders use their 'brilliant brains' in a useful or pure way?

A: *Perhaps some, I think! I hope!*

ON HUMAN EMOTIONS

Q: On transforming fear and despair
Is it possible for an ordinary person to transform his or her fear and despair? How can we do this?

A: *Oh, yes, it is very possible. For example, when I was young I was always afraid of dark rooms. As time went by, the fear went. Also, with regard to meeting people, the more your mind is closed, the greater the possibility of developing fear or feeling uncomfortable. The more open you are, the less uncomfortable you will feel. That is my experience. If I meet anyone, whether a great man, a beggar or just an ordinary person, to me there is no difference. The most important thing is to smile and to show a genuine human face. Different religions, different cultures, different languages, different races – these are not important. Educated or uneducated, rich or poor, there is no difference. When I open my heart and open my mind, I consider people just like old friends. This is very useful. On the basis of that kind of attitude, if the situation is something different then I have the freedom to act according to the circumstances. But at the beginning, from my side, I must create the ground. Then often there is a positive response from the human level. So I think fear is one thing to clear away.*

Also, in the individual's mind there are many hopes. If one hope fails, it does not mean that all hopes fail. I have met some people who tend to feel completely overwhelmed and who become desperate when they are not able to fulfil one of their hopes. But I believe that the human mind is very complex. We have so many different types of hopes and fears that it is quite dangerous to invest everything on one particular hope, so that when that hope is not fulfilled we are totally overwhelmed. That is a bit too dangerous.

Q: On dealing with attachment to material wealth and companions
   You talked about dealing with attachment to our own body. What methods are effective in dealing with extreme attachment to material wealth and companions?

A: *For someone who accepts rebirth or any form of existence after death, there are various sorts of reflections that one can do, such as reflecting upon the ultimate futility of being too attached to one's companions or one's material wealth, or reflecting on the transitory or impermanent nature of these phenomena. One can reflect on how being extremely attached to these phenomena can increase one's afflictive emotions and lead to frustrations and so forth.*

Now even if you are a non-believer or a genuine atheist, then if you look at the purpose of our lives, you will see that life is not simply meant for wealth or for your dearest ones. There are many other purposes. If you are a non-believer, I think you can still conduct certain types of contemplations as a means of reducing your extreme attachment towards material wealth and companions. For instance, you could think that material wealth and companions are definitely some of the various conditions for your happiness and sense of fulfilment, but that does not mean that these are the only conditions or means for your sense of fulfilment or satisfaction. Therefore, there is no point in being single-minded and investing all your energy in this, because it is not the only condition that you require for leading a happy and fulfilling life. In fact, similar types of contemplation can be found in classical Buddhist literature such as Four Hundred Verses on the Middle Way.

Q: On true tolerance
Could Your Holiness speak a little more about inter-personal relationships in accordance with personal karma? How does one understand the difference between tolerance and stupidity?

A: *True tolerance is a stand or a response an individual adopts in relation to a particular incident, or towards another person or event, when the individual has the ability to act in a contrary manner. As a result of one's considerations, taking into account many factors and so on, the individual decides against taking negative action, and this is true tolerance. This is quite different from a situation in which an individual has no capacity whatsoever to take such a strong counter-measure. Then he or she is in a helpless position, so can't do otherwise. The difference between the two is in fact quite clearly pointed out in one of the Buddhist texts known as* Compendium of Deeds *by the Indian master Shantideva. So my tolerance towards the Chinese is actually quite open to question – is it really genuine tolerance or not?!*

Q: On overcoming fear
How may one overcome fear or fearfulness as a habitual state of mind, especially when there is no apparent cause?

A: *I think that the kind of outlook you have and the way you think makes a big difference. Often we find ourselves being hit by a sudden thought or feeling, such as fear, which, if we leave to itself, or, in other words, give in to without paying much attention, can begin to work in its own cause and begin to affect us. It is crucial that when such things arise one must apply one's faculty of reasoning so that one does not fall under the sway of these thoughts and feelings. Of course, if there is sufficient reason to fear, then fear is good! Fear creates preventive measures, so that's good. Yet if there is no basis for fear, then when you meditate analytically the fear will be reduced. That's the proper way.*

Q: On spontaneous compassion
Can compassion arise spontaneously after one has developed direct intuitive insight?

A: *I think it depends very much upon one's own spiritual orientation and the basic motivation. It is possible for certain practitioners who have developed familiarity with various principles of the Mahayana path, altruism and so forth. As the individual gains greater insight into the nature of reality, the greater the power of his or her compassion and altruism will be, because he or she will then see that sentient beings revolve in the cycle of existence due to ignorance of the nature of reality. Such practitioners, when they gain very deep insight into the nature of reality, will also realize the possibility of a way out from that state of suffering. Once you have that realization, then your compassion towards sentient beings will be greater because then you will realize their fate – although they can get out, they are still caught in the cycle.*

But simply because one has gained a certain degree of insight into the nature of reality does not guarantee an automatic spontaneous experience of compassion. This is because one's insight into the nature of reality can be motivated by an altruistic wish to help other sentient beings or it can be induced by a motivation primarily concerned with one's own interest of attaining liberation from cyclic existence. So simply by generating insight into the nature of reality on its own cannot really lead to genuine compassion; you need some additional conditions.

Q: On forgiveness

Can you speak about forgiveness? In my past I have done some wrong and questionable things, and feelings of guilt intrude on my peace of mind, although I work hard to repair the damage I have done. What actions can I take to aid my forgiveness of myself and others?

A: *If you are a practising Buddhist then it may be effective to engage in a form of purification practice which involves the application of what are known as the Four Powers, one of these being a sense of regret for the action committed. This already seems to be present. Another factor that is needed is a sense of resolve not to engage in such acts in the future. Complemented with these two factors, the actual purification practice could involve taking refuge in the Three Jewels and then engaging in certain religious practices, such as making prostrations and reciting mantras, meditating on love and compassion, or meditating on Emptiness, the ultimate nature of reality.*

Q: On the positive expression of anger
Are there examples of the positive expression of anger based on compassion and self-understanding?

A: *Yes, it is possible to have circumstances in which the basic motivation can be compassionate, but the immediate catalyst or motivating factor can be anger, which is a very strong force of mind.*

Q: On dissolving the pain of child abuse
If one is damaged or abused as a child, and in adult life the scars lead to depression and negative emotions, can we dissolve the pain through meditation? And is the process of psychotherapy complementary to the Way?

A: *I think it is best to use both techniques. It may differ according to the circumstances but, generally speaking, they are definitely complementary.*

Q: On staying in touch with your emotions
Your Holiness, how can I stay in touch

with my emotions without being afraid? I often control my feelings so much that I am closed off and unable to love.

A: *When I talk about love and compassion, I make distinctions between the ordinary sense of love and what I mean by love. What I mean by love can arise on the basis of a clear recognition of the existence of the other person, and a genuine respect for the well-being and rights of others. However, love based on strong attachment towards one's close ones is, from the point of view of religious practice, something that has to be ultimately purified. A certain degree of detachment must be developed.*

I think that perhaps at the beginning level you may find some kind of loneliness. Actually, that is one of the aims of the lives of monks and nuns. While in one way that sort of life may seem a bit colourless or unattractive, in another way it is more colourful. In reality, I think the one form of happiness has too much fluctuation, so I think in the long run the other type, although less dramatic, is something steady. In the long run I think that it is much more comfortable! So that is one consolation for monks and nuns!

Q: On dealing with despair and depression
   If someone feels in the depths of despair and, in a very deep depression, lies at night wanting to die, what is your advice to help that person become more stable and positive?

A: *It is very difficult if it is someone who has no background or practice. Then I really don't know what to advise. But if it is someone who has some experience of practice or some other religion, and if he or she has some experience of Buddhist practice, then it is helpful to think about Buddha Nature and about the potential of the human body and the human brain. It is also helpful to read the stories of great practitioners of the past, whose lives illustrate the hardships that people have gone through. For instance, in some cases these great masters were people who had previously had almost no education or people who were depressed and lacked facilities and so forth. But as a result of their determination and confidence in their own potential, they were eventually able to attain high realizations. One must also bear in mind that being depressed and losing hope will never really help to correct the situation.*

Q: On transforming the energy of anger and desire
Your Holiness, you spoke of the wrathful deities. Would you say some more about transforming the energy of anger and desire through Tantric practice. What is the key to such a transformation?

A: *Certain qualifications are necessary on the part of the individual who is capable of transforming the energy of negative emotions like anger and desire into the path. Such an individual must have a firm foundation in the realization of the path of wisdom and method. Based on that, such a person must also have a certain degree of realization of the deity yoga meditation: single-pointedness and also a firm identity and appearance of the deity. Then there are certain forms of activities that one can engage in which could enable the individual to transform these energies, including the wrathful action. In order to take such action, one needs some kind of wrathful motivation, such as a certain anger which is entirely based on karuna or compassion. That also affects swiftness. A satisfactory account would involve a long explanation.*

ON BUDDHISM

Q: On right view and wisdom
Surely right view is the beginning of wisdom on the path. It is not just for religion.

A: *You are correct in saying that right view is not necessarily the special purview of* religion. What I meant by stating that perverted or wrong views are one of the Ten Negative Actions from the religious point of view, is because in Buddhism, when the Ten Negative Actions are counted, the perverted or wrong views refer to disbelief in rebirth, disbelief in the possibility of attainment of Nirvana, and so on. These are definitely unique to Buddhist belief.

Q: On meditation
How can meditation help bring about contentment?

A: Generally speaking, when we use the term 'meditation' it is quite important to bear in mind that it has many different connotations. For example, meditations can be single-pointed, contemplative, absorptive, analytic and so forth. Especially in the context of the practice of cultivating contentment, the type of meditation that should be applied or engaged in is more analytical. You reflect upon the destructive consequences of a lack of contentment and the positive benefits of contentment and so forth. By reflecting upon these pros and cons, you can enhance your capacity for contentment. So if one's understanding of meditation is confined to a mere absorptive, single-pointed state of mind, without the application of the analytical faculty, I don't think that this type of meditation alone can lead to the development of contentment. This is because one of the basic Buddhist approaches in meditation is somehow to engage in a form of practice during the meditative session so that it can have a direct impact on one's post-meditative period, for example on our behaviour, our interaction with others and so on.

Q: On karma
Karma is the law of cause and effect of our activity. What about the cause and effect of inactivity?

A: Generally speaking, when one talks about the doctrine of karma, especially in relation to negative and positive karma, it is definitely linked with a form of action. But that does not mean that there are neutral actions or neutral karma, which can be seen as a karma of inactivity. For instance, if we are confronted with a situation in which someone is in need of help, suffering or in a desperate situation, and the circumstances are such that, by being actively engaged or involved in the situation, you can help or relieve the suffering, then if you remain inactive that can have karmic consequences.

But a great deal depends upon one's attitude and motivation. So irrespective of whether the individual has the capacity to relieve a person from his or her suffering, if the person's attitude is such that he or she is totally indifferent to the other person's well-being and in a way abandons that person's well-being or need, that could definitely have negative karmic consequences. But this is quite different from a situation in which an individual does not necessarily wilfully *disregard others' needs, but rather remains inactive out of a lack of confidence and a lack of courage. That can be seen as less negative.*

Q: On gaining confidence in our Buddha Nature
What is the best way to gain confidence in our Buddha Nature?

A: *Based on the concept of Emptiness, meaning the objective Clear Light, and also the concept of the subjective Clear Light, we try to develop a deeper understanding of Buddha Nature. It's not easy, but through investigation, I think both intellectually and through making connection with our daily feeling, there is a way to develop some kind of deeper experience or feeling of Buddha Nature.*

Q: On the nature of sentient beings and whether plants have Buddha Nature
Your Holiness, modern science cannot make a clear distinction between plants and simple forms of animal life. How

does Buddhism decide who has mind and who doesn't? Would it be possible to believe plants participate in the cycles of existence and have Buddha Nature?

A: *At one of my meetings with scientists on the interface between modern science and Buddhism, the question was raised of how we determine whether a living thing is sentient or non-sentient. Eventually, all of us came to an agreement that the deciding factor is the capacity to move, mobility. Of course, from a Buddhist viewpoint there are other sentient beings who have no form, like those in the formless world. In addition, within the form realm where beings do manifest in physical form, Buddhist literature mentions sentient beings in the shape of plants, flowers and so forth. But as to the specific question of whether or not we can find out whether, for instance, the plant over here is sentient or not, I honestly don't know how to determine it. I think that on a conventional level people think, 'That's just a* plant.' So we accept it just as a plant.

But still, one must take into account that in our perception of reality there are various levels of discrepancy between the way in which we perceive things and the way in which things and events really unfold. This may have some relation to a statement made in a Buddhist philosophical tenet known as Madhyamika Prasangika, which provisionally accepts the distinction between falsity and reality, illusion and reality, but ultimately does not accept such a distinction.

Q: On conscious and subconscious beliefs
In attempting to view life in a positive light, how does Buddhism deal with the dichotomy between conscious and subconscious beliefs?

A: Although I am not very clear about the meaning of the English term 'subconscious', according to Buddhism, when we talk about the means of overcoming various afflictive and negative cognitive *and emotional states, we make a distinction between those which are conscious or manifest experiences and those which remain in the form of dispositions, pre-dispositions or tendencies. Between the two, overcoming the conscious and manifest cognitive and emotional states is considered to be easier than overcoming the subtle tendencies and predispositions of mind. Therefore, in the Buddhist scripture, when presenting the path to Enlightenment, insight into the nature of Emptiness is seen as the counter-force for overcoming the obvious and manifest forms of these afflictive states. It is only through constant familiarity with the understanding of the nature of reality, through a long process of meditation, that one can eventually overcome tendencies and dispositions.*

Buddhist literature mentions various stages in the process of overcoming afflictive and negative states. The first is to train oneself in such a way that at the initial stage the person has reached a level where, even though he or she might come across certain circumstances and conditions which normally would give rise to negative and afflictive responses, due to practice the person will not give rise to these negative states. This will then be followed by a more advanced state in which the person can actually directly counteract and prevent the arising of afflictive emotions. Finally, at a still more advanced stage, the person can actually remove the seed or potential that gives rise to such negative states. So, as you can see, the process of overcoming our negative and afflictive cognitive and emotional states is very complex. It is not just by generating an insight into the nature of reality that, in one instant, you can remove all the negativities from your mind.

To give you some idea of the complexity of the process, we can see that with regard to a particular issue our minds go through states which are quite different. For instance, one's position regarding a particular issue could, at the initial stage, be totally contrary to reality. As a result of trying to understand the exact reality of the situation, perhaps that single-minded misunderstanding can then be slowly questioned and turned into a wavering state, in which you think that maybe it is the case, maybe it is not. That wavering state of hesitation can then, through further analysis, turn into a state of presumption, tending towards the correct conclusion. When further reinforced and familiarized, that state of presumption can be turned into a state of true knowledge. At the initial stage, that true knowledge may only be an inference based on certain premises, and therefore conceptual. But through constant familiarity, eventually that inferential understanding can, according to Buddhism, culminate in a direct, intuitive understanding of the nature of reality. So you can see there is a kind of a progression. This in a way illustrates the complexity of the forces of overcoming our afflictive states. So according to Buddhism, a true state of cessation, in which the individual has totally overcome the effects of *negative and afflictive emotions and cognitive states, is said to be a direct and intuitive insight.*

Q: On why Buddhism is described as a spiritual path
   Your Holiness, why is Buddhism described as a spiritual path when everything revolves around the mind?

A: *Yes, it is true that some people describe Buddhism as a science of the mind rather than a religion. In the writings of one of the greatest Buddhist masters, Nagarjuna, it is mentioned that the approach of the Buddhist spiritual path requires the co-ordinated application of the faculty of faith and intelligence. Although I don't exactly know all the subtle connotations of the English term 'religion', I would personally think that Buddhism can be defined as a sort of combination of spiritual path and philosophical system. However, in Buddhism, greater emphasis is given to reason and intelligence than faith. Yet we do see* roles for faith. For instance, Buddhism categorizes all phenomena into three classes: first, immediately obvious phenomena – those things which we can directly experience, or relate to and understand; second, certain types of phenomena which require inference through a logical process but which we can still infer from obvious premises; and third, phenomena which are called the 'obscure phenomena', which can be understood only by reliance upon the testimony of a third person and, in the context of Buddhism, the testimony of the Buddha. By reliance on Buddha's word we accept their existence.

But even then the testimony of Buddha is not taken simply on blind faith just because he is the Buddha, but rather because Buddha's word has been proven reliable in the context of phenomena and topics which are amenable to logical reason and understanding. By inferring that Buddha has been proven reliable in these matters, one can then conclude that Buddha's word can also be taken as valid on issues or topics which are not so immediately obvious to us. So there is a kind of a role for faith there, but still we can see that it ultimately depends on reason and intelligence or one's understanding. So Buddhism can be described as a combination of a philosophical system and a spiritual path, or, rather, it can be seen as a combination of a mental science and a spiritual path.

One of the reasons why I say that in Buddhist methodology, especially in Mahayana Buddhist methodology, greater emphasis is placed on reason and understanding, is because we find in Mahayana Buddhism a distinction between two different categories of Buddha's words. Certain types of Buddhist scriptures can be taken as literal and definitive, and certain types cannot be taken at their face value, are not accepted literally and require further interpretation. How do we determine whether a certain type of scripture is literal and definitive or whether it requires further interpretation to determine the *meaning below the surface? That can be done only by reliance on a form of reasoning. So ultimately understanding and investigation are the judge. This spirit is very clearly illustrated in Buddha's oft-quoted statement: 'Bhikshus and wise men do not accept my words just because they are the words of the Buddha, simply out of reverence for me, but just as a goldsmith would test the gold through various procedures and then finally make a judgement, similarly accept the validity of my statements only after you have subjected them to analysis and investigation.'*

So in a way Buddha gave us liberty to carry out further investigation of his own words. It seems that among humanity, one group of people describe themselves as radical materialists and another group base themselves solely on faith, without much investigation. Here are two worlds or two camps. Buddhism belongs to neither one. From one side Buddhism is a science of the mind, so that one side rejects it, saying it is not a religion. From

*the other side, Buddhism is too spiritual;
it involves meditation and things like
that, so that other side rejects it. Thus
Buddhism remains between the two.
Perhaps that's one advantage: we can
work as a bridge to bring these two
extremes together. Sometimes I feel that
in the future there may be an important
role for Buddhism in bringing both sides
together.*

Q: On celibacy
   Is celibacy required for Enlightenment?

A: *I think generally not. Yet you may ask
why Buddha himself eventually became
a monk. I think, from the viewpoint of
the Viniya Sutra, the main purpose of
celibacy is to try to reduce desire or
attachment.*

   *From the viewpoint of Tantrayana,
particularly the Highest Yoga Tantrayana, the energy, 'drops' or special
bliss is the source of energy to dissolve
the grosser level of consciousness or the
grosser level of energy. Through experi-*

ence of that special bliss, there is the possibility that the grosser level will eventually dissolve. So the drops are the key factor for the bliss.

In Tibetan Buddhism, especially if you look at the iconography of deities with their consorts, you can see a lot of very explicit sexual symbolism which often gives the wrong impression. Actually, in this case the sex organ is utilized, but the energy movement which is taking place is, in the end, fully controlled. The energy should never be let out. This energy must be controlled and eventually returned to other parts of the body. What is required for a Tantric practitioner is to develop the capacity to utilize one's faculties of bliss and the blissful experiences which are specifically generated due to the flow of regenerative fluids within one's energy channels. It is crucial to have the ability to protect oneself from the fault of emission. It is not just a purely ordinary sexual act. And here we can see there is a kind of special connection with celibacy.

Especially in the practice of the Kalachakra Tantra, this precept of protecting oneself from the emission of energy is considered to be very important. The Kalachakra literature mentions three types of blissful experience: one is the blissful experience induced by the flow of energy; one is the immutable blissful experience; and one is the mutable blissful experience. To me, when Buddha took the celibacy vow, at that level he did not explain all the reasons behind that rule or that discipline. The complete explanation comes when we know the Tantrayana system. Perhaps that answers your question. So, I think the answer is both 'Yes' and 'No'!

Q: On women and celibacy

The answer you gave about the need for celibacy and use of bliss and non-emission was from a man's point of view. Why is a woman's part in these practices never mentioned? What does a woman need to do with her energy to gain Enlightenment through bliss?

A: *It is the same technique and the same principle. According to some of my Indian friends, practitioners of Hindu Tantrayana also realize the practice of kundalini and chandralini. My information is that the female also has some kind of energy, drops. So it is the same method.*

Q: On the form of our rebirth
Who or what determines what we come back as?

A: *According to Buddhism, it is karma, one's own action, that really determines rebirth. Also the state of mind at the point of death has a crucial role. Those who have some familiarity with Buddhism may already know that there is a principal doctrine taught by the Buddha known as the 'Twelve Links in the Chain of Independent Origination'. The second link in the chain is karma. However, the presence of karma alone is not sufficient to lead to a rebirth, therefore circumstantial conditioning factors* such as afflictive emotions and cognitive events are necessary. These are the eighth and the ninth links, which are attachment and grasping. So when the karmic imprint is activated by the force of the eighth and the ninth links, attachment and grasping respectively, then the karmic imprint becomes mature, which is the tenth link, known as the link of becoming. So the nature of one's rebirth basically depends upon the karmic imprints and potential of the individual being, not only accumulated during the present life but also during his or her previous lifetimes. Also, within the karmic potentials there might be some that are more forceful or powerful and some which are less powerful. Abhidharma Kosha, a Buddhist text, mentions that among the 'karmic potentials' or 'karmic seeds' that one might possess within one's mental continuum, it is the most forceful one that would determine the nature of rebirth. And if the individual has many equally strong forces of karmic imprints, then it is the karmic action *which is closest to the present life that would come into fruition. And if there are still many karmic imprints of a similar nature, then it is the karmic action which the individual is most familiar with that would lead to fruition and determine the next rebirth. As I mentioned yesterday, one of the determining factors or conditions is the state of mind at the point of death.*

Q: On using the dream state
Could you say more about using the dream state?

A: *It is only in the highest Yoga Tantra, Tantric Buddhism, that we find meditative techniques that can be applied during the dream state. There are two main purposes for such types of meditation using dream-state consciousness. As I pointed out yesterday, it is during the dream state that we have an opportunity to rehearse or become familiar with the processes of dying, because there is a kind of an analogous process of dissolution* experienced during the dream state. In a way, meditators rehearse by utilizing the dream state so that they can become familiar with the dissolution processes and train themselves to be able to recognize the various signs that are associated with various levels of dissolution.

But the principal purpose of dream meditation is to train oneself in such a way that, even during the dream state, the individual can actually experience what is known as the Clear Light, the most subtle level of consciousness, thus enabling him- or herself to actually experience dissolution of various elements during the dream state. And for that you require the capacity to recognize dreams as dream states. There are two principal methods for doing that. One is through Prana Yoga, which is the practice of the energy channels and which is quite an advanced method and is difficult for beginners. The other method is not so much through the practice of Prana Yoga, but rather through developing a sort of a determination or mental force –

developing a strong will to identify or recognize dream states as dream states. It also has many connections with the type of diet you adopt, your behaviour and so on.

Q: On the recognition of women in Tibetan Buddhism

Why has there not been any recognition in Tibetan Buddhism of women on the level of lamas or gurus?

A: *Actually there are some very high reincarnate institutions, like Samdring Dorje Phagmo, that traditionally are women lamas of a very high position. The current Samdring Dorje Phagmo Lama is the fourteenth incarnation. This demonstrates that this institution seems to be as old as that of the Karmapa, which is considered the first reincarnate institution in Tibet.*

So there are a few reincarnated female lamas. Of course, the majority, both now and in the past, are male. One must admit that in the past, the position of women may have been neglected or not given much thought. Part of the reason for this negligence of the rights and position of women within Tibetan Buddhism is because in the past people simply did not give much thought to it. We more or less took the status quo for granted. For example, I recently had a meeting in Dharamsala with some Western Buddhist teachers during which a point was made that in the ordination ceremony there are instructions about how to determine the seniority of ordination and that the custom seemed to really reflect a bias. At the meeting I promised that within six months I would organize a big conference, at least among our Tibetan scholars and bhikshus, to discuss these things.

Overall, I think that in the Buddhist system, especially in the Viniya Sutra, men and women both have the right to the highest ordination, the bhikshu and the bhikshuni. Yet it is also a fact that the bhikshu remains higher and bhikshuni lower. Then in Bodhisattvayana, *everyone is believed to have the same Buddha Nature. In addition, the capability of achieving the level of Bodhicitta and of practising the six paramitas is exactly the same.*

Now, regarding the exact Buddhist stand on the issues of gender, discrimination, women's rights and the position of women in Buddhism, as I pointed out earlier, as far as the presence of Buddha Nature is concerned, there is no difference. Nor is there any difference in terms of the potential that an individual has for generating the highest altruistic aspiration to attain Buddhahood or insight into the ultimate nature of reality and so forth.

But one must accept that there is certain Buddhist literature which does reflect a kind of discrimination. For instance, in one of the texts, Abhidharma Kosha, in which certain characteristics or features of an advanced level of Bodhisattva are mentioned, one of the characteristics seems to be that the person who is on an advanced path

towards Enlightenment is in the form of
a male practitioner. So it does seem to
reflect some bias. But if we were to look
at the issue from what I see as the
highest stand-point of Buddhism, which,
according to our understanding, is the
position of the Highest Yoga Tantra, I
would say there is no discrimination
based on gender, because in the practice
of Highest Yoga Tantra you first of all
require initiation into the practice, and
initiation of Tantra is not complete
without the full, equal participation of
both female and male practitioners. For
instance, both male and female can
receive empowerment. Also, in the deity
yoga mandala, the full participation of
both male and female deities is necessary. And where Tantra is concerned,
there are in fact specific precepts for
Tantric practitioners which say that if
you belittle or disparage a woman it
constitutes an infraction of a Tantric
precept. Similarly, on the path, full experience of the Tantric path towards
Enlight-enment can come about only

if there is a complementary practice between both male and female practitioners. For example, if the practitioner is male then he requires assistance, a stimulus, from the opposite sex; and similarly, if the practitioner is a female, she requires assistance, a stimulating factor, from the male practitioner. This touches upon the topics we discussed about the generation of blissful states of mind; but this is completely different from ordinary sex. Similarly, both female and male practitioners can become fully Enlightened in their form as males and females. So from the stand-point of Highest Yoga Tantra, I would say there is no difference or discrimination based on gender.

I think it's very important for women to try to appropriate all their rights. Among the Tibetan refugee community in India, I have for many years been advocating for the female side, the nuns' side. They must have the interest or courage to study as the monks do. While at times in Tibet, almost none of the nunneries were places of serious study, there are legends of a different past in which there were nunneries which were important centres of philosophical learning and debate, so much so that there were several cases of debates between monks and nuns and the monks lost! So you see, for more than 20 years in India I have been continually making an effort for the female side, and they also must take the full initiative – that's important.

Q: On determinism
Some people and teachers say that when you perform an act or make a decision, it is not really you making that decision, and what is meant to happen will happen regardless of the fact that you thought you made the decision or had an effect on some activity or situation. If this is so, how do we create karma, if it is not really us making the decision?

A: *I think that is the wrong conception. If this sort of fatalistic account of our actions and existence is true, then the very idea of the possibility of liberation or Enlightenment simply would not make any sense. Because the idea of Enlightenment entails that we completely change our karma and that salvation or Buddhahood is achieved. It is an entirely new initiative, which never happened in the past. That is exactly what is meant by practising, embarking on a spiritual path. I mentioned earlier that sometimes people, including Tibetans, use karma as a sort of excuse. I think that's wrong.*

Q: On meditation without purification of motivation

About great harm when meditation is practised without purification of motivation: I have met people who have achieved some power of the mind and use this power with a selfish, even cruel, motivation, with their minds crystallized or blocked and their hearts literally hard or impure. Is there any method of de-crystallization of energies fastened together in a wrong way?

A: *What is important is to have a very balanced approach in one's meditation. In fact, because of this significance in Buddhist teachings we often talk of 'comprehensive path'. For instance, if someone were to concentrate solely on generating insight into Emptiness without paying much attention to the development of the more compassionate aspects of the mind, then that can in fact result in a lower path. Similarly, if one puts all one's concentration on the development of the compassionate factors of the path, without paying any attention to the wisdom and intelligence aspect, then one's altruistic aspiration and attitude can never be really fully enhanced because they will be lacking the complementary factor. So generally one could say there are two distinct approaches in an individual's practice of the Buddhist path. One is engaging in a Buddhist practice of the path based on the development of understanding of the entire framework of the Buddhist path and how most of the key elements fit within a certain framework. However, there could be another approach which could be seen as more individualistic, in which an individual may not have a full understanding of the entire general framework of the Buddhist path, but simply follows single-pointedly an instruction given by an experienced master. Then the master is really extremely important and must be really qualified. That is then some exceptional case, without extensive study.*

Q: On blind faith
What do you feel about blind faith in order to reach Enlightenment?

A: *I don't think one can get far!*

Q: On compassion and the dependence of others
Your Holiness, in trying to be a compassionate human being, how responsible should we feel? What should you do if you find someone emotionally dependent on your compassion? Is it compassionate

to hurt someone if you think it is the best in the long run?

A: *I think you should keep in mind compassion with wisdom. It is very important to utilize one's faculty of intelligence to judge the long-term and short-term consequences of one's actions.*

Q: On the significance of the actions of one individual
I can understand how my own mind and actions can affect my own causes and conditions. Can they also affect world conditions like hunger, poverty and other great sufferings of beings everywhere? How?

A: *Sometimes we feel that one individual's action is very insignificant. Then we think, of course, that effects should come from channelling or from a unifying movement. But the movement of the society, community or group of people means joining individuals. Society means a collection of individuals, so the initiative must come from individuals. Unless each individual develops a sense of responsibility, the whole community cannot move. So therefore it is very essential that we should not feel that individual effort is meaningless – you should not feel that way. We should make an effort.*

Q: On whether beginners should proceed slowly or quickly in learning Buddhism Would you advise Western beginners on the Buddhist path to proceed slowly and cover less ground or to try to learn as much as possible and proceed faster?

A: *Again, it depends on the individual case. I think in some cases extensive study is more suitable or useful. But it is important to keep one thing in mind: you should realize that spiritual development takes time; it doesn't happen just overnight. Perhaps some lama may say, 'Oh if you follow my teaching you will gain some spiritual experience within one week or two weeks.' I think that's nonsense.*

Q: On Clear Light mind
Your Holiness speaks of an innate Clear
Light mind. This appears to come from
Dzogchen discourse. In fact, the concept
of an innate mind is the object of refuta-
tion by the *Madhyamika Prasangika*
dialectic. Some Gelugpa hierarchies have
even considered the Dzogchen tenet to be
heretical and non-Buddhist. Yet Your
Holiness has developed a way to integrate
these two seemingly contradictory views
of ultimate nature. Could you explain
how Dzogchen is compatible with Lama
Tsong Kapa?

A: *First, I think you have made a mistake.
Perhaps there might be some confusion
here between two sorts of apparently
quite similar but actually very different
concepts. On the one hand there is
innate Clear Light mind, and on the
other, what I have referred to as 'innate
grasping at an enduring self'. These are
two different things. Innate grasping at
an enduring sense of self is in fact still at
the conceptual level where the thought*

processes are still active. That's when the innate grasping of self still operates, whereas innate Clear Light mind becomes manifest only at the most subtle level. But by that time much of the conceptual thought processes have already ceased their functioning, so these are two different things.

But as to the actual nature of Clear Light mind, whether it is still conceptual or non-conceptual, there are divergent opinions. Another difference is that Clear Light mind is being generated inside to perceive the nature of reality. In fact, this is one of the most powerful attitudes for overcoming the grasping at an enduring notion of self. It is stated that when the objective Clear Light, which is the Emptiness conjoined or assimilated with the subjective experience of Clear Light, which is the one innate mind that is being referred to here, the most powerful awareness to counteract the force of grasping is realized. I think when we talk about Gelugpa's position or standpoint we have to identify that more with Lama

Tsong Kapa, the founder of the Gelugpa tradition, and to his two main disciples. We find that in one of the writings of Khnanpuje, one of the two foremost disciples of Lama Tsong Kapa, a question was raised as to the authenticity and efficacy of the Dzogchen view of ultimate nature. Khnanpuje says that so far as the actual view of the ultimate nature of Dzogchen tenets is concerned, it is an authentic view, something that can be definitely applied in one's practice of Highest Yoga Tantra. But the reason why there has been criticism of the Dzogchen view is because some of the Dzogchen practitioners around that time seemed to demonstrate a certain degree of laxity towards ethical principles.

But one thing we have to bear in mind here is the usage of the term 'view' – the right view – the view of Emptiness. In the Madhyamika literature, when the view of Emptiness is mentioned, the reference is often more towards the object of Emptiness, the nature of reality as it is, whereas when this term 'view' is used in the Dzogchen terminology and Mahamudra literature, then the reference is more to the subjective experience rather than the Emptiness. This distinction is quite important and it must be appreciated, because if we compare the view of Emptiness between Sutra and Tantra from the point of view of the understanding of Emptiness itself there is no difference. But a difference does emerge from the subjective point of view in that the Tantric subjective experience of Emptiness is said to be more profound.

Q: Your Holiness, if you could have three wishes, what would they be?

A: That is top secret!

ON VARIOUS ASPECTS OF DEATH AND DYING

Q: On accidental or sudden death
Your Holiness, what may happen to one who dies in an accident, such as in a car

accident or by murder and so on?

A: *Under such circumstances, the individual may find himself or herself in a state of extreme anxiety or shock, but generally speaking, the state of mind in such situations can be described as neutral – neither virtuous nor non-virtuous. One thing that I've noticed among the findings of researchers who have done investigations into the phenomena of rebirth based on the testimony of children who claim to recollect their past lives is that in many of the cases, the manner in which the previous life's death was met was quite sudden, like accidents and so forth. So I feel there might be something here which needs a lot of research. From a Buddhist viewpoint, as far as I know there is no particular explanation.*

In India about 10 years ago I met two girls, one from the Punjab and one from Uttar Pradesh. In both cases, the girls had had sudden deaths in their previous lives. One of these small girls had a truly remarkable memory of her past life. As a result, even her parents in her previous life accepted this new young girl as their own daughter, so in fact she has four parents! I began to wonder whether there might be some connection. First, both were female in this life and in their previous lives, and second, both had died suddenly. Perhaps the woman's mind is clearer! I don't know! If that is the case, I think in future there may be more reincarnation among females!

Q: On differences between a peaceful and a sudden or violent death
Your Holiness, please could you speak about any differences which may exist between a peaceful death and a sudden and violent death?

A: *Of course, from the practitioner's viewpoint the natural death is better. There is more time to think and to practise. Also, according to Tantrayana, there are indications when different elements absorb. If the body is relatively strong, these indications of the dissolution of the different* elements are clearer, so the practice becomes easier. If, however, the dying person has had a long illness and has become very weak physically, then the indications may not be very clear. There are certain types of meditative techniques in Buddhism known as 'transference of consciousness', to which a meditator is recommended to apply only as a last resort, and which enable the individual to go through the dissolution processes consciously and with awareness. Prior to that there are various types of indication that could help the meditator ascertain the certainty of his or her death. When these indications keep repeating and there is no possibility of reversal of the eventuality, then the meditators can turn to the last-resort practices like transference of consciousness. But the process of natural death is much better.

Q: On preparation for death and the comatose state
   If someone has prepared well for death,

does it matter if he or she is in a coma up to and at the point of death? Will such a person still have the clarity of consciousness you mentioned as important?

A: *Although it's very difficult to judge the difference between the two states, if I were to guess perhaps I could say that, even though an individual might be a trained meditator, if he or she remained in a state of coma then perhaps it might affect his or her ability to discern the various indications of the dissolution processes. Although at the time of the actual dissolution process, the discernment is not really the same as the gross conceptual state of ascertainment that we normally experience, still the conscious will to discern the dissolution signs does have an impact and an effect on one's ability to remain aware at the time of death. Ideally it would be nice if we could do some experiments on this phenomenon and see, for instance, whether the ability of a trained meditator suffering from physical illness and*

*in a coma to remain in a Clear Light
state was affected or not.*

*Actually, some years ago in Dhar-
amsala a team of scientists came and
carried out some experiments. They
wanted to investigate the process of
death, so they brought one simple
machine. But who can say who will die
when? And who will have an experience?
Nobody can predict this! It is a problem.
Since that time there have been more
than a few cases in which, after death,
the bodies have not decayed. I think in
some cases it has been for up to a week
and in other cases for longer periods. But
when those instances took place, nobody
could conduct an experiment. Yet when
the scientists were visiting with their
equipment, nobody died! That is one difficult job!*

Q: On being HIV positive and dealing with
anger and death
Your Holiness, as someone who is HIV
positive, I find that anger at my state
stops me from working at looking at

death with equanimity. What can help with this anger?

A: *That is a problem. To a large extent society's attitude is also not very healthy because there is a tendency to marginalize those with HIV. In addition, the people themselves are completely discouraged or have a very low state of mental strength. But if individuals have some sort of practice, like Buddhist practice, then of course they can see that this life is just one life and that the end of this life is not the end forever. Also, every event and experience of this life is, of course, due to our own action or karma, not necessarily in previous lives but also due to action within this lifetime. According to the law of causality, these unfortunate things are due to one's own previous actions. So that is also a consolation I think.*

I have met some Tibetan practitioners who have told me of their experiences. Some patients suffering from terminal illness ask for their doctor's honest opinion as to whether their illness can be cured or not, and if their illness is terminal, how long do they have to live. Once these patients know that they have only a certain amount of time left, they say to me that it comes as a kind of relief, because then they can re-orient their lives so that they can get their priorities right. So I think a great deal depends on one's own practice. Other than that, I don't know – it's difficult.

Q: On euthanasia
In cases of agonizing terminal illness or injury, would you condone an assistance to death or mercy killing?

A: That is also very complicated. Again, much depends on the individual case. From the Buddhist practitioner's viewpoint, since these situations are due to past karma or one's own action, sooner or later one has to go through these painful experiences. In such cases, it is better to have pain with this human body, because at least there are nurses

193

and doctors who can take care of you. If it happens in some other form of life, there is no such facility and then the same experience is really hopeless. So this is one way of looking at it.

On the other hand, if one is in a state of coma and there is no hope of recovery, and if one remains like this for a long period, it is very expensive, and the expense may create some other problems. Such a complicated situation may perhaps be an exceptional case, but this is very difficult to say or to generalize. I think one has to decide based on individual cases.

Perhaps one could see some parallels between the practice of mercy killing and the Buddhist practice of transference of consciousness, the difference being that in one case the transference of consciousness is practised upon oneself. There is also a difference in objectives. In the case of mercy killing the motive may be to relieve the individual from extreme pain and agony, whereas in the case of transference of consciousness, it is more to do with granting the individual the opportunity to utilize the occasion of death before his or her bodily elements reach such a stage where the indications of the dissolution process may not remain vivid. So there might be some similarities.

Q: On dealing with pain at death
Has Your Holiness any advice on dealing with pain at the time of dying?

A: For someone who is a practitioner, at such moments it is possible for the effects of one's practices to have positive results, but otherwise it is very difficult to say what can actually be of benefit at that time. That's why, from a young age, these methods or practices are useful, no matter whether the individual is fully qualified or not. One should familiarize oneself with them, so that when the time comes one can deal with these things without much effort. That is the proper way. If one believes that, until the serious situation happens, one does not need to take the practice seriously, then when things become really desperate, it is very difficult and too late.

A great deal depends on how familiar you are with certain types of practice. For instance, if you are quite well trained in various techniques, such as meditation on love and compassion, meditation on the 'identitylessness' of phenomena, and meditation on the impermanent nature of existence, and you have practised giving and taking – giving one's prosperity, happiness and so forth to others and taking upon oneself others' suffering, pain, etc. – then at the time of death you could either reflect upon each training of mind in turn, or you could pay special attention to a particular form of practice. And because of your former familiarity, you will be able to place the main part of your mind or consciousness on the practice to such an extent that it would make even physical pain or suffering less obvious, and pain would affect you less. Similarly, if your power of concentration is great, then you can in fact focus on the *very point where you have pain and then meditate on special practices, like visualizing white light or subtle drops or certain objects or mantras or whatever on that specific point, and that would help reduce the physical pain. But if you lack such familiarity and training, then it's very difficult to judge what could be the best method to overcome pain at that moment.*

Q: On karma and prolonging life unnecessarily
Following what you have said about karma, if one is in a healing profession, what are the karmic responsibilities regarding interfering or preventing the death process from taking place, or prolonging life unnecessarily?

A: *Generally speaking, I don't see any contradiction between a health professional helping a patient to remain alive and the karmic responsibilities involved in it, because when we talk of death, from the Buddhist perspective, it is experienced as* a result of many factors, not just karma alone. There would be a death experience as a result of karmic consequence, for instance, if the karmic potentials have been exhausted; or sometimes the death can be an untimely one, as a consequence of circumstantial conditions; and in some cases, death can be experienced, not because of the exhaustion of full fruition of a karma, but because of an exhaustion of the meritorious potential. Similarly there are different types of illness: karmically caused illness versus illness for which the primary condition or cause is more external or more internal.

The karmically caused death refers to situations in which, in spite of all possible means of preventing it, death cannot be avoided. Generally speaking, that type of experience of death is considered karmically caused. Moreover, in the case of sudden death, where the conditions can be seen as more external, even then karma plays a role. For instance, in the case of prolonging someone's life, the very fact that it is possible to prolong it or that there are conditions for prolonging it, is in a way a consequence of karma.

Actually I have noticed, even among Tibetans, that sometimes people as individual human beings do not take the initiative and that they use karma as a sort of excuse. I think that this is absolutely wrong. Who creates karma? We ourselves, by our actions, create karma. For example, if I want to write something down, that very action creates new circumstances and causes some other result or event. It is cause and effect, cause and effect. To think that karma is some sort of independent energy is wrong! Our daily lives, our good food or good work, our relaxation – everything is through action. It is all action and result, action and result. Whose action? Our action! Sometimes I think that there is some kind of misunderstanding when we talk about karma.

Even if you have already accumulated some negative karma, you still have the opportunity to change or to overwhelm that negative karma by virtuous karma. So everything depends on our own action. That is important. As a Buddhist practitioner, it is very essential to know that. A true practising Buddhist will have conviction in the existence of Buddha Nature, which allows the possibility of attaining the fully Enlightened state, a state of perfection. If that is the case, then why can't the individual have the conviction that he or she can overcome various problems?

The theory or doctrine of karma involves a lot of complex issues, so it is impossible to merely generalize and say that everything is a product or consequence of karma. For instance, in the case of my present physical body, like my hand here, the fact that this part of my body is so intimately linked with my experience and my physical sensations of pain and pleasure is very evident. But if we were to trace the physical cause of this particular part of my body, we could trace it back to the beginning of time. It *is a material phenomenon, or a product of a material phenomenon, which can be traced to an earlier state and an earlier state and so on, until we reach a state in which it is a pure atom or particle. According to Buddhist literature that particle is technically called a 'space particle'. So as a result of this process of evolution throughout billions of years, that minute particle has now fully evolved into this animate physical body which can act as a basis for the arising of sensations of pain and pleasure. So the fact that this body is my body may be seen as a result of karma, but the fact that this body is a consequence of the beginningless continuum of material particles cannot be seen as a product of karma; it is simply the law of nature. Material objects come from material sources.*

Similarly, when we look at the difference between mind and body, we find that there are certain central features that distinguish the two. For instance, material phenomena have certain features that make them physical or material. They are obstructive, whereas mental phenomena have the nature of clarity, luminosity and knowing, but they are not physical; they are not obstructive. The fact that these two exist in such a contrasting or different way is simply a law of nature. We cannot say it is because of karma that they are two different things.

Mahayana Buddhist literature takes this complexity of reality into account and shows that there are different ways of approaching the nature of reality. Buddhist literature mentions four principles for understanding the nature of reality. One is the principle of logical inference, which can be applied on the basis of our understanding of the ultimate nature of reality, but which can be applied only if there is a certain causal connection or interrelatedness between phenomena – the fact that something can give rise to something else or that when certain things aggregate they can result in a certain outcome. On the basis of that principle of dependence we can apply logical inference.

And then that principle of dependence is possible because, for instance, matter and mind, or matter and consciousness, enjoy a different status of existence or different characteristics. The fact that there are such differences is simply a law of nature and in the Mahayana Buddhist literature, that is known as the principle of Natural Law. Taking into account this complexity of the nature of reality, we have to approach an understanding of the nature of reality by many different avenues of reasoning. So determining the influence of karma is difficult. Although we can say that a lot of the things that we experience are products or consequences of karma, determining how far the karmic influence reaches and how much is a consequence of the mechanisms of the natural law is open to dispute. It is something that we should examine and understand, but it is very difficult.

Q: On facing the death of friends
Your Holiness, you face your own death
with ease and peacefulness. How about
the death of your friends?

A: *I don't know. With regard to my own
feelings, yes, sometimes I am very sad – I
was particularly sad when my immediate elder brother, Lobsang Samten,
passed away. I think among my sisters
and brothers, he was the brother whom I
spent the most time with when I was
young, especially when I came from my
birthplace to Lhasa. I think the journey
took over two months. Do you know
about palanquins? There was a small one
and we two brothers sat in it. We were
very playful and when we both went on
one side of the palanquin, the whole
thing tilted. Then the person who was in
charge of it would immediately shout
from the outside, 'Don't do that! Don't
do that!' For him, the best thing was if
we two brothers quarrelled; then we had
a clear demarcation: I sat here, he sat
there. Then the thing was more bal-*

anced! The person who looked after that palanquin wasn't very happy I think! So when my brother passed away, I really felt extraordinarily sad. But then, that is a fact. Since his death I have occasionally wondered, 'Oh, where is his rebirth? In this world or in some other place? If it's in this world, where?' Sometimes this feeling comes.

Q: On the intermediate state of mind between death and rebirth
You described an intermediate state of mind between death and rebirth. Is this linked to any kind of physical or biochemical processes, or is it independent of physical processes?

A: *The fact that such an intermediate state has no connection or link with the present body is quite obvious according to the texts. It is described in the texts that such a being has a body which is by nature subtle energy, not a corporeal body, but it is also described as possessing a type of colour and shape. An analogy used in describing the body of the intermediate state being is that of a dream body. It is said that some advanced meditators can, during the dream state, actually assume a dream body, and that body is said to be very similar to the body of an intermediate state being. A dream body can naturally be experienced by some individuals, whereas some individuals can deliberately attain it.*

You have asked about subtle energy, or some aspect of subtle mind. Yet you see colour and sometimes shape. It is a complicated matter, but it seems to me that there are the external five elements and the internal five elements, and within the internal, there are the grosser level of the five elements and the most subtle elements. In the most subtle base, there is Clear Light. Clear Light is one aspect; another aspect is the subtle energy. In that energy there is some kind of seed of the five elements. So when we discuss the Clear Light as a foundation of all existence, I think there is some link with external, solid things and Clear Light. There is a mention of a particular energy force in the Tibetan Buddhist literature technically called the Energy with Five Radiances, and I think some connection can be seen between the macroscopic world of our everyday experience and the microscopic world of subtle energy. The link which is provided between the two can be understood by understanding the nature of this particular energy force which is mentioned in the texts. What is so crucial here in furthering our understanding of this connection is to see whether there is any significant relation between this particular energy force and what I have described as the space particles. I myself do not have as yet a fully developed idea.

Q: On knowledge of death and the *Tibetan Book of the Dead*

Is the knowledge of the processes of death to be formed by reading the *Tibetan Book of the Dead*?

A: *Yes, it is helpful. As for the process of death, particularly the various features and characteristics of the intermediate state, we sometimes find sort of divergent presentations in the Abhidharma literature and the Tantric literature. So perhaps it is best to try to have a broader understanding by reading more texts. However, most of the visualizations and the visions that are described in the* Tibetan Book of the Dead *may be considered more specific to a particular practitioner of deities known as the mandala of the wrathful and the peaceful deities as mentioned in that text.*

ON THE SITUATION IN TIBET

Q: On dealing with Tibet and a large non-Buddhist Chinese population
If you returned to an independent Tibet, would it be difficult to reconcile the Buddhist principles of compassion with the reality of governing a state with a large Chinese non-Buddhist population?

A: *I have already noticed during the last few decades so much degeneration in Tibetan culture and the Tibetan way of life. Besides our Chinese brothers and sisters, even among Tibetans it seems there is some danger. Take, for example, some young Tibetans who have escaped from Tibet in the last few years – although their sense of being a Tibetan is strong and very good, certain aspects of their behaviour make me grow more anxious. They immediately fight or use force and, in recent months, there have been two murder cases involving young Tibetans who have escaped from Tibet. Every other aspect of their motivation is excellent, but there is so much degeneration in their humbleness or honesty and compassionate attitude. So even in India among our own people, these kind of things are happening. Due to these recent events I have really developed genuine concern. What is really happening inside Tibet, my country?*

But then that's reality, so we have to face it. Still, I believe that when we have freedom – freedom of speech, freedom of thought, freedom of movement – we can minimize these things. Although in the future, when we have freedom, I will no longer be the head of the Tibetan government. That is my final decision. In fact, we have made an official document that says that as soon as I reach a free Tibet, we will form an interim government and I will hand over all my legitimate authority to that government. Within two years, that government will organize the Tibetan People's Assembly. Then it will decide the Tibetan constitution. So that is something that is already decided.

Q: On His Holiness' future role in Tibet
Your Holiness, you said earlier that the changing attitudes of some of your Tibetans makes you anxious. So I wondered why you have decided to give up your historic authority in Tibet when it would seem that young people need spiritual rather than political guidance.

A: *The fact that I will no longer be the head of the Tibetan government does not mean that I will give up my moral responsibility or commitment. Of course, being a Tibetan, particularly since I am so trusted, it is my obligation to serve, to help humanity in general and particularly those people who very much trust me, till my last breath. In fact, the one reason why I do not want to carry the responsibility of government is that, after all, I am already 57, so I consider that I have about another 20 years of active life; then I will be too old. In any case, within the exile community in India we are already stepping up the democratic system. Within the next 20 years, democracy must be established. Otherwise at the initial stage there may be turbulence, disturbances or complications. All these complications should occur within my lifetime and then in the future things may go more smoothly.*

    Also, if I continue to carry the responsibility, although I think many Tibetans might appreciate this, indirectly it would become an obstacle for the healthy development of democracy. Therefore, I decided I must be out. There is another advantage: if I remain as the head of the government and a problem develops between the Tibetan central government and local people or an administration, then my presence could lead to further complications. If I remain as a third person, then I can work to solve such serious matters.

Also, personally, I do not want to be involved in ceremonial things. I don't like them and it's an extra burden. I would like to have more freedom to move here and there without any protocol. It is much easier and better, isn't it? For these reasons I have made my decision. But this does not mean that I will give up my responsibility or my commitment.

Q: On using violence to free Tibet
Your Holiness, wouldn't sacrificing your beliefs in using violence to free Tibet be a worthwhile action, as this would result

in the alleviation of suffering of the Tibetan people?

A: *No, I don't think so. In that situation, more violence would happen. That may lead to more publicity and that may help. But after all, the most important thing is that China and Tibet have to live side by side, whether we like it or not. Therefore, in order to live harmoniously, in a friendly way, and peacefully in the future, the national struggle through non-violence is very essential.*

Another important matter is that the ultimate agreement or solution must be found by the Chinese and Tibetans themselves. For that we need support from the Chinese side, I mean from the Chinese people's side; that is very essential. In the past, our stand was the genuine non-violent method; this already creates more Chinese support, not only from the outside but inside China also. There are more supporters amongst the Chinese for our cause. As time goes on, more and more Chinese are expressing their deep appreciation and their sympa-thy. Sometimes they still find it difficult to support the independence of Tibet, but they appreciate our way of struggle. I consider this to be very precious. If Tibetans take up arms, then I think we will immediately lose this kind of support.

Q: On support for Tibet
What would your Holiness like the members of the audience do to help the Tibetan cause?

A: *Although I am very, very encouraged to receive great support from many differ-ent places like the United States and here in Britain, we still need more active support. You see, the Tibetan issue is not only a human rights issue, it also involves environmental problems and the issue of decolonization. The most important issue at present is the ques-tion of Chinese population transfer. At this moment we need more support to stop this demographic change. This is very, very crucial. Whatever way you can show support, we appreciate it very much.*